The Courageous Choice

An Amish Family's Shattered Dream

Mary Schrock
Author of The Greater Inheritance

ISBN: 978-1-946598-29-5
Truth Book Publishers
www.truthbookpublisher.com

First Printing 2021

Cover design by Rosa Balzamo

All scripture is quoted from the King James Version

ACKNOWLEDGEMENTS

A heartfelt thank you and deep appreciation to my daughter, Rosa Balzamo, who willingly worked countless hours editing and polishing the manuscript and designing the cover. Without her sacrifice of much time, patience, and encouragement, this book may not have become a reality.

I'm also genuinely grateful to my husband John and our other four adult children and their families for praying and encouraging me to persevere when writer's block hit numerous times throughout the process.

Last, but not least, I give all praise and thanks to my Lord and Saviour who led and guided me in writing this novel which is based on some very real and true happenings in my own life and in the life of some Amish friends. My sincere desire is to see others experience the liberating love and grace of God available to them.

One
CHAPTER 1

Rosanna took a deep breath to calm her racing heart as she quietly slid into her antiquated desk in the Amish one-room schoolhouse and glanced at the clock. *If only I could become invisible for the next half hour and then come back as an ordinary eighth grader! Why didn't I slip out the door faster this morning! It's not fair!*

In a long, flowing Amish navy dress, a bonnet, and a shawl, with a lunchbox in hand, Rosanna had been ready to begin her one-mile trek to school earlier that morning. But Mem (Mother) had stopped her at the door with a reminder to always set a shining example for her classmates.

"If teacher Martha calls on you to lead a song during the opening song session this morning, I want you to choose a German church hymn. I know you'd rather sing the faster school songs, but singing an occasional drawn-out church hymn would be even better. As one of the older students, it's important that you encourage the younger ones to make wise choices," Mem smiled proudly.

Rosanna paused with a nod, but had no time to plead for mercy before she hurried down the sidewalks. Seeing her siblings were already several hundred feet ahead of her, she soon dismissed the thought of trying to catch up with them as she pondered over her mem's disturbing instructions.

The other students always get to choose what they sing. Why do I have to stand out and be the odd one again? What if I mess up the song? They might even make fun of me.

The rock in the pit of her stomach and her anguished heart became heavier with every step as she walked along. She feared losing her breakfast by the roadside. *Maybe I could avoid the frightful situation if I told teacher Martha I'm not feeling well. I wouldn't be lying. But, I'm sure Mem would not forget, and it would only postpone the command.*

The school bell rang soon after Rosanna and her siblings had arrived. Singing was first on the morning agenda.

Rosanna had a glimmer of hope after the first few songs that she might not be on the singing schedule that morning. Alas! After the next song, teacher Martha paused as if looking for a suitable person to lead the closing song. *Oh no, please not me! Not this morning!* Rosanna held her breath.

"Rosanna, would you lead our last song, please?"

Teacher Martha's gentle voice sounded like a thunderclap to Rosanna's ears and anxious heart! Every fiber within her trembling body wanted to scream, *NO!* But her conscience would have tormented her the rest of the day had she disobeyed her mem. So she nodded at teacher Martha. She refrained from bursting into tears as she flipped through the pages in the back of the book in search for the shortest hymn available.

Rosanna cringed, fearing her singing voice might tremble or falter. When she announced the page number, all heads turned towards her as if she had made a mistake. She kept her eyes glued on the page as she led the hymn in her soft, beautiful voice. Leading a German church hymn was even more intimidating than she had imagined.

When the last verse ended, her trembling hands slapped the song book shut as she fought back tears of fright and embarrassment. She breathed a quick sigh of relief after it was over, and no one had even sneered at her. Teacher Martha's kind smile of approval soothed her flustered heart.

It's just like teacher Martha to show such compassion and understanding. No doubt, she also has experienced the results of the teaching that "children are to be seen, not heard."

* * * *

In the beautiful spring days of late April, Rosanna was excited to graduate from eighth grade. She had completed her education according to the Amish traditions and now looked forward to learning practical life skills at home.

Over the next few years, she enjoyed many opportunities to help other families in the community. Busy mothers would often need help with their large family or a big workload. Working for a mother with a newborn was her favorite job away from home. As the oldest daughter, she was the first in line for the job. She was no stranger to hard work.

Her days of independence and freedom to make her own life's decisions had only begun. But she soon found it difficult to give up that freedom when she returned home from a job.

I'm sixteen now. Shouldn't I be able to make a few of my own decisions? Did Mem forget I'm not a junior girl anymore?

She felt a tinge of guilt, knowing rebellion toward her parents was not pleasing to God. Rosanna soon sensed her intention to be the compliant daughter would not be a smooth path. Nor could she have imagined the future conflicts and heartaches she would experience on her journey of life.

One day in early autumn, Rosanna grabbed her black bonnet to accompany her mem to their local Amish fabric store. When entering the store, it surprised Rosanna to run into her best friend, Emma. She now saw Emma only at church since they had both graduated in the spring.

The girls browsed through the store as if in a dream, admiring the wide assortment of beautiful fabrics stacked on the shelves. Rosanna ran her fingers over an elegant light blue fabric as she envisioned herself dressed in its beautiful color.

"That color would look lovely on you reflecting your pretty blue eyes," Emma commented.

"I'll be lucky if I can convince my mem of that," Rosanna said.

By the time Emma's mem had made her selections of fabrics, Rosanna and Emma had seen most of the supplies in the store. For a moment, Rosanna wished to be Emma's sister as she observed Emma's mem make her purchases. Emma smiled at Rosanna as she followed her mem out the door.

Rosanna sensed the cocoon of covetousness tightening around her heart. *Emma is so fortunate!*

Her bitter envy inspired her to grab the bundle of light blue fabric recommended by Emma and at least attempt it - "Look at this blue fabric, Mem! It's on sale, and I'd need only about three and a half yards for a dress. Seems it would be acceptable since Bishop Yoder's girls wore dresses of this color at church a few weeks ago," she said, as she held the fabric up for her to examine. Rosanna held her breath as she watched her mem's expression. *Would her appeal be convincing enough to secure her wish?*

Mem took it to the daylight coming through the window and examined it from every angle.

Rosanna waited in suspense. At last, Mem handed it back to her.

"I feel it is questionable, and a little lighter than I want my daughters to wear. To keep on the safe side, we need to stay with darker colors," she said, deciding against it once again. She reminded Rosanna of how important it is to abide by the church rules and help maintain the Amish traditions.

"The bishop is in charge of our church rules, and his own daughters wear those dresses. Doesn't that mean it's allowed by the church, or are they disobedient?" Asked Rosanna.

"It is not disobedience, but I believe it would crowd the boundaries. When in doubt, we should make the safer choice; there is also the danger of a prideful heart when wearing such light colors," said Mem.

Rosanna's heart sank as she left the store without the lovely fabric she had hoped to get this time to make a beautiful dress. She left with her mem's choice of a darker blue fabric. Rosanna felt that her limited selection of dark brown, black, navy, and medium blue dresses were boring compared to her friends' wider variety.

Mem's attempted conversation starters on the way home did nothing for her daughter's sullen mood - except make it worse. Rosanna's head was churning hundreds of frustrated thoughts like a rock tumbler.

Why does living righteously and following the rules have to be so complicated? Does the color of my dress even matter to God?

Rosanna looked forward to the day when she would be of age at twenty-one, according to Amish standards. *Then, I can make my own decisions and purchases.* She already imagined the pleasure of choosing those colors which were favorites even at a young age. Widening the range of colors would enhance her wardrobe while violating no church rules.

During the next several snowy winter months, Rosanna continued to practice her sewing skills by making her own clothing and various items for the family. This relieved Mem from some endless sewing tasks.

However, Mem's monitoring and peering over Rosanna's shoulder was disheartening. Mem felt it was her responsibility to ensure Rosanna's measurements of the hem width, apron bands, collar heights, and *kopp* (head covering) strings, to name a few, were precisely within the church guidelines. Guessing the measurements was not acceptable on Mem's sewing machine.

Rosanna despised being the odd-ball family of the community who unconditionally and flawlessly complied with the church guidelines.

Why don't other families have to be perfect? Are we better than they are in God's eyes? Do we have a better chance of heaven than they do if we're impeccably blameless?

Rosanna's bedtime prayer often included asking God's forgiveness for resenting her mem's pursuit of excellence. Yet, without a doubt, she knew it would happen again. She was right!

Two

CHAPTER 2

By the following spring, Rosanna had perfected her sewing skills to the point of being able to cut out and stitch together a new prayer *kopp* for herself in a hurry. She enjoyed sewing in peace while her Mem was away for the day. Yet, she was still careful to follow the rules in order to pass Mem's inspection when she came home.

However, despite her diligent efforts, the next Sunday morning when Rosanna ran upstairs to prepare for church, she eagerly pulled out the girls' *kopp* drawer. She picked up her new crisp and neatly pressed Sunday black *kopp*. Turning it over, she wanted to admire her skillful handiwork one more time before putting it on her head.

Instead, her heart sank in utter dismay when she noticed that Mem evidently had made a secret inspection run when Rosanna was not in the house. By hand, Mem had altered some of the carefully pressed *kopp* pleats to assure compliance with the church rules.

Now, Rosanna was no longer in a worshipful mood as she blinked back tears of frustration. She was certain she had violated no church rules while sewing or pressing it.

Minutes later, when her fourteen-year-old sister Laura walked into the room, she immediately knew by the look on Rosanna's face that her day was not going as planned. Laura was not surprised at what had happened, and she understood her sister's frustration all too well. "Remember how Mem always likes to go above and beyond for good measure," she reminded Rosanna.

"I know, but why do we always have to be the goody-two-shoes who follow the rules more perfectly than everybody else? Does God even care what my *kopp* looks like, just as long as I'm wearing one? Is it any wonder we are often mocked and ridiculed? Why can't we just be an ordinary Amish family?" Rosanna asked in exasperation.

It didn't help matters when Mem demanded that Rosanna and her sisters exemplify humility by going to church barefooted on warm summer days. Rosanna and Laura were embarrassed to be the only barefooted mid-teenage girls in church.

An hour later Rosanna was sitting with the other girls her age on a hard wooden church bench. Her bare feet were promptly tucked out of sight underneath the bench. She had finally calmed down enough to at least appear to be listening to Bishop Yoder's preaching. She assumed it would be many of the same quotes and remarks that she had heard the last time.

Then, suddenly as he preached, Bishop Yoder caught her attention when he admonished the congregation about the sin of rebellion. "The Bible says in 1 Samuel 15:23, *For rebellion is as the sin of witchcraft…*" he quoted.

Rosanna hung her head in guilt. *I know it's wrong to rebel against my parents, but life is so difficult and unfair. Lord, forgive me and help me live pleasing to you. I need your help right now.*

Her heart was still heavy with discouragement when the service had ended. Bishop Yoder had provided no biblical solutions to her problems. Rather, he encouraged the congregation to be more diligent in abiding by the church rules and traditions.

Meanwhile, she tried to smile and appear to be a happy barefoot girl sitting under the shade tree with her friends, waiting to be called to the table for the traditional after-church lunch.

She was glad when her two brothers, David and Ben, were finally ready to go home after lunch. The rest of her family would leave later.

After they arrived home, the boys went to their rooms to nap. Rosanna was thankful for the privacy as she entered her own room and closed the door. She flung herself across the bed as she let go of all her pent-up emotions of the day and sobbed uncontrollably. Her heart was dangling between the struggle to live "righteously," and the fierce desire to fit in with her friends. Either way, she felt doomed and hopeless.

At last, she drifted off long enough to catch a short but refreshing nap before the rest of the family came home.

* * * *

A few days later, Rosanna rode to town in the buggy with her dat (dad). While he shopped in Hayden Hardware, she browsed in the gift shop next door.

Since she was still frustrated from the events of the previous weekend, she was not even aware that it had weakened her resistance to temptations.

There it was on the top shelf! A beautiful harmonica, just like the one her friend Rhoda had in secret. She could almost hear the lovely sound coming from the irresistible shiny instrument.

Take it? Or leave it? She disliked on-the-spur- of-the-moment decisions. But she must get back to the hardware store in a few brief minutes. She picked it up, then put it back down. ... *obey your parents… against the church rules… terrible girl… it's sin… you know better!*

However, she ignored that annoying whisper gnawing at her conscience. *Just once can't be that bad, can it?* She persuaded herself that the pleasure of fitting in would be worth the consequences.

She snatched it off the shelf again before she'd change her mind. Taking it to the checkout, she nervously handed over her precious babysitting money. After quickly tucking her prize into her dress pocket, she hurried back to the hardware store.

In her excitement with her secret purchase, she had not anticipated the nagging pangs of guilt which tormented her on the quiet ride home. Dat was a man of few words. *But if he only knew…*

By the time they arrived home, she doubted the wisdom of her impulsive decision. She dreaded to think of the consequences if someone discovered it. *How will I ever get out of this unscathed? Will it tarnish my reputation forever?*

CHAPTER 3

Early one morning the next spring, Rosanna's oldest brother David, who was of age but not yet married, stopped by asking for help on his farm. For the past few months, he had been living on the farm which he rented from Bishop Yoder. It wasn't long until he had learned he needed help to manage all the farm chores and field work.

Rosanna would love to work on her brother's farm! She expected Dat would need nineteen-year-old Ben's help at home, therefore he could not help David.

Her mind immediately started racing as she developed a strategy. She realized it would require some time and ingenuity to persuade her Mem, but she was determined to get the job.

Before David left, Mem promised him she would talk it over with Dat when the guys came in from the field for lunch.

As Mem mentally analyzed the situation, she didn't see how Dat would spare Ben, and the thought of letting Rosanna go didn't comfort her either. She assumed Levi would be too young.

Mem kept herself busy at the sewing machine all morning, while Rosanna and her siblings worked in the enormous vegetable garden behind the house. It was important to keep the weeds from getting out of control.

Rosanna realized a beautiful garden full of hardy vegetables and pretty flowers were every typical Amish lady's pride and joy. However, Mem's garden was different. It did not display pretty flowers to enjoy and beautify the garden. She would allow only vegetables, melons, and other family favorites to be planted. Mem believed flowers were an unnecessary work and a potential source of pride.

But Rosanna admired the many beautiful flower gardens throughout their Amish community. She enjoyed every opportunity she had to study her book on growing rose bushes. She could almost smell them right off the pages. Already, she had visions of caring for her own gorgeous rose garden someday.

Soon Dat and the boys came in for lunch. As the steaming bowls of meat, potatoes, and vegetables circled around the table, Mem informed Dat of David's request for summer help on the farm.

After they had discussed several options, Rosanna carefully offered to fill the need. She reminded them how much she enjoyed working with horses and the farm machinery.

Dat needed all the boys at home during the summer, so it would only make sense to let her help David, she explained. She also reminded Dat that her younger sisters could help Mem in the garden. She could even come home for a day if they needed her help, she said.

Her parents glanced at each other as they considered the options. Rosanna held her breath, hoping her simple reasoning was convincing enough to land her the job. After finishing his plate of food, Dat suggested they think it over and wait until evening to decide. *That's so typical of Dat. Never in a hurry,* thought Rosanna.

During the afternoon, Rosanna encouraged each of her siblings to help convince their parents they could manage the chores, garden, and other work in her absence during the summer.

At chore time that evening when Dat brought his team of horses in from the field, Mem met him outside the barn as he unhitched them.

"What are we going to do about helping David this summer?" she asked, out of earshot of the children.

"It seems logical to send Rosanna if you will spare her. But since you depend a lot on her help around the house as the oldest daughter that may not be the best idea," he said.

"Well, with some extra effort from the younger ones, we could manage without Rosanna's help," said Mem. "However, I'm concerned about sending her away from home all summer. She isn't a church member yet, so the temptation of taking advantage of her independence might be too much. She might still need a little supervision to follow the rules, especially with her love for sewing her own clothes."

"Yes, I know what you mean," Dat said. "Levi is fifteen now and has proven himself capable of most responsibilities around here. So it would seem Ben is best suited for the job. Maybe Rosanna could take Ben's place in the field here at home whenever needed."

"It would be less worrisome to send Ben. He can cook too," Mem smiled.

"But not like Rosanna," Dat chuckled as he followed the last horse into the barn.

Mem hurried back to the house to help prepare the evening meal. After finishing the chores, they enjoyed eating together around the family dining table, and sharing about the events of the day.

Rosanna wasn't very talkative as she waited for Dat to announce their decision about helping David. The suspense was almost killing her.

Dat casually finished his dessert, with no hint of their decision about helping David.

Minutes later she was disappointed when everyone left the table with no mention of it. Her mood slumped as her hopes were fading. *How could they forget? Should I remind them? No, I might be nagging, and produce negative results.*

She helped clear the table and wash the dishes, while her mind was bursting with curiosity. *Would they allow me to go help David on the farm?*

At last, as Dat reminded everyone it was bedtime, he turned to Ben, "Better get a good night's sleep since you will help David on his farm tomorrow."

Ben stopped short with one foot already on the bottom step of the stairway. *What! Is Dat serious?* He wondered as he turned to listen.

"What about Rosanna?" Ben felt sorry for her. He knew she had her heart set on getting the job.

Dat explained to them that it's just better to let Ben help with David's farming. Then, turning to Rosanna, he said, "I'd appreciate your help occasionally in Ben's place in the fields at home whenever you have time to help." She only nodded.

After Ben received the instructions and a few details of the plans, he raced his brothers up the stairs, too excited to fall asleep immediately. He wondered what all his summer adventures might entail. He was not used to an independent life.

With great disappointment, Rosanna closed the book she was reading and slowly climbed the stairs to her room. She wanted to respect her parents' decision. Yet, a turmoil of questions plaguing her mind kept her awake late into the night.

Why wouldn't they allow me to go help David? She could think of only one reason. *Was it possible they have learned about my secret instrument? No, I would have heard about it immediately.*

Someday I'll dispose of it when…. At last sleep overtook her.

In the following weeks, staying busy helped silence the nagging whisper disturbing her guilty soul. *Sin… rebel… disobedient… doomed.* It kept tormenting her heart every idle moment.

The circle of new friends resulting from her secret had gradually opened several attractive doors of opportunity for her. To her surprise, walking through those doors wasn't as fulfilling as she had envisioned. The pretense of happiness; lack of peace and joy; fear of dreadful consequences; fear of eternal damnation; broken parental trust. Those were the ugly monsters awaiting her beyond the enticing doors of sin. *Repent before the doors are locked behind you!* The whisperer tormented her.

Four
CHAPTER 4

Rosanna had almost grown accustomed to the unsettling twists and turns of her mid-teenage years, when she faced an unusual twist.

It surprised her one summer afternoon when a car with a California license plate pulled up in front of their house.

"Who is it, Mem?" Rosanna asked. She could not imagine what someone from California would want at their house. And she had no idea how her life was about to change forever.

Mem peeked out through the door window. *Why did he look somewhat familiar? Could he be that worldly cousin of mine?* Mem wondered. *If so, the children wouldn't need to hear they had a relative who drives a car and dresses like a heathen,* she thought.

The older boys and Laura were working outside, but she quickly instructed the younger children to stay in the living room, away from the front door. She asked Rosanna to supervise them.

Then Mem answered the door with hesitance.

"Hi, you must be Lydia?" the man answered.

"Yes, I am," she replied with a smile.

"I'm Clemens, your Uncle Jacob's son from California," he beamed!

"Oh, yes, I remember Uncle Jacob and Aunt Lizzie. I'm sure you miss them since they're gone," she said.

"Yes, I miss my parents, but I'm glad to have my brother, Harvey close by."

They exchanged some more awkward chit-chat, but she didn't feel compelled to invite him to step inside since she assumed he was an Amish outcast.

"So, what are you doing living in California?" She asked.

"I am one of the business managers of a manufacturing company in San Diego. I was just coming through this area since I occasionally take business trips for the company," he said.

"Sounds interesting. I've never been to California, but isn't it a rather worldly place to live?" she asked, shaking her head.

"Yes, it is, and truthfully, anywhere we go, there is worldliness all around us. But we have to remember who the 'world' is in the biblical sense."

"What do you mean? Isn't it those who wear flashy clothes, have modern conveniences, drive cars, and live to please themselves?" she asked.

"Honestly, the Bible definition of 'the world' is speaking of those who are not a child of God, according to 1 John 2:15-17 and also 1 John 5:4-5," Clemens clarified.

"Many of them don't even go to church," she added. "I suppose you go to church, the way it sounds?"

"Oh, yes!" Clemens assured her. "I love the Lord, and I'm a member of a Baptist church there in San Diego. I also serve in various church ministries."

"Baptist!" she exclaimed in shock. "So you believe their false teachings of a 'know-so salvation'? Doesn't that seem rather boastful?"

"My Bible tells me, by faith, I can know I have eternal life. Through Christ's sacrifice on the cross for my sins, I have received His forgiveness! I'm reconciled with Him," Clemens explained.

"So, now you can live however you want, huh?" she asked.

"Oh, no! As God's child, I now want to live for Him and serve Him because He gave Himself for me. Doing right doesn't make me a child of God. It marks me as a child of God after I have become His," he said.

"Are you telling me wearing worldly clothes and driving a car is living for God? Seems that is contrary to the way a follower of God ought to look and live. We believe in Jesus, too. But, you might remember from your Amish upbringing, that our understanding of faith involves many things. Some of which are humility, abiding by the church rules, and keeping the traditions of our forefathers."

"Yes, I remember those teachings. And I'm neither proud of, nor ashamed of my background. It was just a part of the lifestyle into which I was born. But I believe differently now," he said.

Mem ignored his remark as she continued. "Do you keep God's commandments and do you observe communion and feet washing as Jesus did?" she quizzed him further.

Rosanna's ears perked up when she heard Mem ask those questions! Curious how the visitor would answer, she tiptoed closer to the living room door, while carefully remaining out of sight.

"Lydia, let me remind you we can not earn salvation by our own deeds, or even by keeping the commandments. It is His gift to all who repent and receive Him. The Bible says in Ephesians 2:8-9, *For by grace are ye saved through faith; and that not of yourselves, it is the gift of God. Not of works lest any man should boast.* I have nothing to boast of myself since Christ did it all. He paid for my salvation in full. I can add nothing to it. I must repent of my sins and unbelief and receive His gift to me," Clemens said.

What? How can he say that? Is that in the Bible? Rosanna's mouth dropped open as she listened. *Maybe I shouldn't be eavesdropping, but I can't leave now, I need to know more.* Her head spun like a merry-go-round.

"Do the ladies of your church wear a prayer cap?" She heard her mem interrupt.

The tone of their lively conversation quickly rose several decibels as Mem firmly defended her position concerning the vitally important and fundamental Amish tradition -- the prayer *kopp*!

By then, Clemens realized it was time to move on. His futile attempts to enlighten his cousin through Scriptures was apparently a mutual waste of time. Or was it?

He had no way of knowing that Rosanna had overheard something which she could never erase from her mind!

Clemens asked briefly how the family was doing, and received the standard reply that all was well. Then, with a cordial goodbye, he returned to his car.

Turning onto the dusty gravel road leading to the highway, he didn't deny the disappointment and sadness he felt in his heart. It reminded him again of the depth of spiritual darkness in which his Amish relatives ignorantly chose to live. He realized that only the power of the Holy Spirit could enlighten their blinded eyes and hearts.

"Dear Lord, draw these dear people to Yourself, open their eyes to understand Your Truth…" he prayed from a burdened heart.

Rosanna was not the only one brimming with curiosity. The visitor was barely out of earshot when her siblings emerged from the living room with a blast of questions for Mem.

"Who is he?"

"Did you know him?"

"Why did he dress like that?"

"Is he a bad guy?"

"Children! Children! One question at a time!" Mem exclaimed as she tried to calm the chaotic scene.

"He was from another state and wanted to stop by to visit. Now, hurry on to finish your work, so you can go down to the creek to play before chore time." She hoped the surprise break would distract them from asking any more questions.

With their questions forgotten and excited about getting some free time, they rushed outside to finish their work!

"Rosanna, how are you coming along with sewing those new curtains for the upstairs windows?" Mem asked.

"It is going well. I have only four left to sew, then I'm finished with that big project." She enjoyed the sewing which didn't require any precise measuring and had no rules to follow except the color of the fabric.

"Who was the out-of-state visitor who just left?" Asked Rosanna, reminding Mem of the question asked earlier by her siblings.

Mem turned to look out the window. She was uncertain how much information she wanted to reveal about her worldly cousin, and wished she would not have to explain the sad reality. Rosanna's curiosity about him also disturbed her a little.

"Oh, that was my cousin Clemens from California. He was coming through here on a business trip," she said, turning back to Rosanna.

"So you have non-Amish relatives?" Rosanna asked. "I never knew that!"

"Yes, I'm sad to say, that is true. It is such a shame that some forsake their precious Amish upbringing to join a world of sin and hopelessness. Oh! God forbid that any of our children should ever make such a foolish and wicked choice. I could not imagine anything worse ever happening to our family," Mem added.

Rosanna realized Mem and Dat were only one of the many Amish parents who hoped to avoid ever having to suffer the disgrace and grief of a family member abandoning the fundamentals of their Amish faith and traditions.

"It is dangerous to associate too closely with such wayward people, so we do not want to welcome them freely into our homes," Mem continued.

"He says, he believes in Jesus; but, by the looks of him and his lifestyle, one has to wonder, where is his evidence of Christianity? Always remember what the ministers teach us... we must not only have faith, but our lifestyle ought to prove it."

"Yes, I know," Rosanna said, barely listening as she sat in deep thought. Her eavesdropping had provoked some disturbing questions, which she didn't dare ask anyone. She almost regretted having overheard it. Yet, she was greatly intrigued.

I must repent and believe to receive His gift to me? Her mind could not escape those words she had heard. Clemens had said it with such confidence. But what about our church rules and traditions?

Five

CHAPTER 5

Early that fall, when Rosanna turned seventeen, she joined the church youth group of boys and girls her age and older. She enjoyed her first Sunday evening at the youth singing where many of her church friends welcomed her. They all sang together in unison.

Soon after the singing, her brother David and the other dating couples left for the girlfriends' respective homes. Their dates would last a couple hours, or until their allotted time expired according to the church rules.

Rosanna's cousin Rudy dropped her off at her house on his way home since he had no girlfriend yet. He forewarned her it probably wouldn't be long until one of his friends would ask her on a date.

"Rosanna," he paused, looking at her in the dim light of the buggy lantern, "always remember this - you are not obligated to accommodate everyone who shows an interest in you. But some guys can be persistent, as you may find out."

"Oh, I don't think you need to worry about me," she chuckled. "There are plenty of girls around who are far more popular than I am." She was thinking of her family's ultra conservative reputation, which would not be attractive to many young men.

"We'll see! Good night," Rudy said and smiled as he slapped the reins on his horse's rump and drove off into the darkness.

Rosanna was well aware of the courtship rules her parents had established for their family. A man who wanted to seek her friendship must commit to purity and adhere to church regulations and traditions. She assumed that in the dating aspect, her parent's stance would be to her advantage.

Yet, she could never have imagined the complicated dating experiences she would encounter on her journey to the marriage altar.

After a few months, Rosanna began to feel comfortable in the youth group. Then, as her cousin Rudy had predicted, her life was about to take another surprising turn.

It was a cold Sunday evening in December when Rudy's friend Jacob was the first to ask Rosanna on a date. She hesitated, not knowing his family very well. However, she nervously consented to let him take her home and visit for a couple hours.

The next morning her parents were more than eager to find out who her visitor had been. Rosanna assured them he was a respectful guy and the visit had gone well. However, Mem could not resist reminding her to always be certain her date is a man of character and strong in the Amish faith and traditions.

Over the next few months, Rosanna was stunned when Jacob was not the sole contender for her friendship. Paul and Eli were also competing for her attention. She assumed she had plenty of time to make a wise choice since she knew her parents would not allow her to get married before she was twenty-one years old.

However, by springtime Paul had become rather persistent in pursuing a friendship with her and had captured her heart. Rosanna felt honored to hold the attention of a man of his caliber. He also charmed her with his pleasant personality. She was certain that her parents would approve of him.

Along with joining the youth group and dating came the expectation to join the class of baptismal candidates that spring. Consequently, in late April, she joined two other girls and three boys for their first instruction class to prepare for their baptism in August.

She found, however, that it was very intimidating to sit in front of five or six preachers for thirty to forty-five minutes in the bi-weekly class they were required to attend. The private room where they met was often small and crowded. Because the church service began at the same time, they could frequently hear the rest of the congregation singing in another part of the house.

It especially delighted her parents that Rosanna desired baptism and church membership. However, after the first several classes, Clemens' words echoed increasingly louder from the recesses of her mind, *Salvation is a gift... repent and believe... receive it...*

Ever since Clemens's visit the previous summer, Rosanna had tried to suppress her curiosity and confusion. Yet, she couldn't forget the confidence with which he spoke. But she began to realize it contradicted some teachings she had been receiving in her baptismal classes.

Each Sunday, she looked forward to their afternoon family nap times. But instead of napping, her mind was under attack. She spent those private moments studying the Bible in search of answers to the millions of confusing questions bouncing around in her head every day. After an hour of trying to make sense of it all, she plopped her Bible onto her dresser.

How should I expect to understand the scriptures with no one to help me? Asking for help would cause suspicion. Even my parents would label me a rebel. It would devastate them to have their daughter questioning the preachers. She shook her head, trying to clear her mind from frustration.

Maybe Clemens was wrong! That would be a simple answer! She entertained those thoughts for only a few minutes. But no matter how hard she tried to convince herself of that, her doubts and questions persisted.

If only I could talk to Clemens again, I would ask him to clarify some things. But what were the chances of ever running into him again? Slim, since he lives in California.

Two weeks later, on Monday morning after an especially disturbing class the previous day, Rosanna was in the washhouse mindlessly hand-feeding the clean wet clothes through the wringer of the washing machine before hanging them outside on the clothesline to dry. She let her mind wander as she worked. Not only was she daydreaming about her visit with Paul the previous evening but also about the confusion growing within her soul.

Suddenly, Bruno began barking, interrupting her daydreaming. Looking out the open door, it surprised her to see Emma and her mem coming in the driveway. After tying their horse to the hitching post, Emma stepped into the washhouse while her mem went on into the house.

"Good morning," Rosanna greeted her over the roar of the gas-powered engine. "What brings you here this early in the morning?"

"Hi, Rosanna! Well, Mem has a dentist appointment today, so we are making it a shopping day which we don't get to do often," Emma smiled. "You look bright and perky this morning! I'm guessing you had a wonderful date with Paul last evening," she winked.

"Yes, we had a good evening," Rosanna smiled. "I don't deserve Paul, but he has been such an encouragement to me already! He is all I've ever wished for in a special friend!" She paused, remembering she had not intended to let any guy smite her heart so soon, much less verbalize it!

"I'm sorry, Emma, I don't mean to sound all mushy already. But you are a faithful friend, and I feel that I can share my heart with you."

"Oh, I understand, and I'm so happy for you! How are the baptismal classes going by now?"

Rosanna had hoped no one would ask. She wasn't sure she wanted to take the risk of letting even her best friend know what was on her mind. But she had to get some advice from someone.

"Well, I've been having a troublesome time making sense of some things," she choked out the difficult words. "I just don't know..."

Just then, both of their mems emerged from the kitchen door onto the open porch, still chatting about the apple butter recipe they came to pick up.

"Looks like Mem is ready to leave. Can we talk more about this next Sunday after church?" asked Emma, bursting with curiosity and concern.

"Sure," nodded Rosanna.

"Enjoy your shopping," she said, as Emma and her mem climbed into the buggy.

Rosanna turned to go back into the washhouse and picked up the last load of clothes to hang outside. She wondered what it was like for Emma to have an entire day for shopping and have money to buy things. It seemed she enjoyed the perfect teenage life.

Rosanna remembered that she had seldom been to town until she had reached the age of thirteen. Her parents tried to protect their younger children from worldly influences as much as possible and avoid the risk of developing ungodly desires.

CHAPTER 6

The next Sunday, Emma waited impatiently for the church service to end. She couldn't imagine what was disturbing Rosanna about the baptismal classes.

At last, after what seemed like a day instead of three hours, the service was over. It didn't take Rosanna and Emma long to find a private spot behind the house.

"What is it?" Emma asked anxiously.

Sitting on the lush green lawn, Rosanna nervously tugged on a blade of grass. "I don't even know where to begin, or how to tell you what troubles me. I should probably talk to my parents first before I talk to you, but since you asked…"

"As your friend, I'm here to listen and help you in any way I can," Emma interrupted.

"I appreciate that, Emma, but I'm not sure anyone can help me," she said as Emma watched her face intently, waiting for her to continue. "It's just that… um... well, I'm not enjoying the classes anymore like I used to, and I'm confused.

"What are you referring to?" Emma asked with a furrowed brow of concern.

Rosanna continued, "Our parents and the preachers have always taught that we must abide by the rules and traditions of our church. And we must do our best to live right if we hope to earn a home in Heaven someday. They talk about it in every class. But, not so long ago, I heard some contradictory interpretations of those Scriptures from someone who says he is a Christian. I can't seem to get his words out of my mind, and I'm not sure who to believe anymore."

"I'm so sorry to hear that, Rosanna! Who told you something different, and what did they say?"

"It was one of my mem's relatives who left his Amish upbringing many years ago. He said salvation is a gift and by receiving it, we can be saved as he called it. This may sound too simple to be true, but he was quite knowledgeable about the Bible," said Rosanna.

"First of all, the fact that he left our circles of beliefs and teachings and is living out in the world is enough proof that he is on the wrong path. We have to be very careful who we listen to, especially if they contradict what our parents taught us," warned Emma.

"But what if he is right and we are wrong?" Rosanna asked in desperation. "I wish I could meet him again and just ask him to clarify it for me. Possibly I misunderstood him."

"Remember to be careful, Rosanna. False teachers are everywhere. We need to trust our forefathers' teachings, which they have passed down for many generations."

"I know, but I would like to understand what he meant."

"Lunch is ready!" Emma's younger sister exclaimed as she came running around the corner.

"Thanks for listening, but don't mention it to anyone else, please," whispered Rosanna.

"I won't, but I'll be praying that you'll find peace."

Rosanna was glad to go home right after lunch. She needed some time alone to think and sort things out in her troubled mind.

The following week Mem reluctantly agreed to let Rosanna spend Thursday, Friday, and Saturday helping David on his rental farm in the peak of the season. David and Ben struggled to keep up with the busy pace of farming along with taking care of all the animals. As Rosanna also cooked their meals and took care of their laundry, she imagined herself doing that for her future husband some day. *Would it be Paul?*

On Friday morning, when David and Ben had scarcely left for the field, a car came in the driveway, surprising Rosanna.

"Not an old salesman," she muttered. She immediately pretended no one was home. That always seemed to work for her mem.

When she heard the car had stopped in front of the house, she carefully peeked out the window. *A California license plate? A salesman from California?*

When the gentleman stepped out of the car and started towards the door she realized she had seen him before somewhere.

What!... Her heart racing, she ran to the door and opened it before he knocked.

"H- Hello," he stammered, with a surprised expression. Why did this young lady not wait for him to knock? He had remembered the Amish women to be rather shy in opening the door to strangers.

"Hi," Rosanna greeted him excitedly. Then, before he could respond, she asked, "Are you Clemens?"

"Y-Yes, I am," he answered and nodded. "But how did you know me?" he asked, totally mystified.

"Good to see you! I am Rosanna. My mem is your cousin Lydia. You have not met me before, but I remember when you stopped by to visit with Mem last summer," she blurted out, forgetting her shyness.

"Oh yes," he exclaimed, remembering that visit. "I was just coming through here on a business trip again today. But what a coincidence that I stopped here to ask for directions to the Dutch Furniture Shop! Without a name on the mailbox, I had no idea who lived here, but God did!"

"I also stopped at your parents' house, but apparently they were not at home. Nobody answered the door." Secretly, Rosanna wondered where her mem and siblings were hiding this time.

"I don't think your visit is an accident, Clemens!" Rosanna exclaimed. "Ever since you visited with my mem that day, I have had some questions which I never expected to have an opportunity to ask you. But God answered my prayers!"

"Ah, yes! The Lord knows how to plan such things," Clemens answered with a chuckle.

She smiled and continued, "You didn't know I was eavesdropping on your conversation with my mem when you stopped at our house. She tried to protect us from your influence. Even now, she would be alarmed if she knew you were here."

"Oh, then maybe I should leave soon?" he asked.

"No, no! She doesn't come here often, so I don't think you need to be concerned," she quickly assured him.

"I had no idea you were eavesdropping that day, but I hope I didn't cause you any trouble."

"No, I didn't dare tell anyone I overheard part of your conversation. But that day you told Mem with such confidence about salvation being a gift and how we just have to receive it. I've been so confused ever since hearing that, and I need to understand what you meant by the gift of salvation."

"Rosanna, I'd be more than happy to clarify it, but I don't want to get you into trouble."

"No, don't worry about that! My brothers are in the back field, and there is no one else around."

Rosanna glanced toward the road, making sure the way was clear before she continued.

"I am also in the baptismal class at church this summer. But in my confusion, I'm not even sure at this point if I want to continue. I need some answers before I can go ahead with the baptism."

Immediately, she nearly gasped. *I can't believe I just said that to someone I barely know! I hope he won't tell anyone.*

However, Clemens didn't seem to notice her alarm as he continued.

"Rosanna, they are merely teaching you what their parents and many generations before them had taught them. The Amish standard of judgment is primarily their traditions and secondarily the Bible. However, we must always ask ourselves, what does the Bible say?"

"God's Word is very clear, there is only one way to Heaven, and it is through Jesus Christ. We can't earn eternal life through our own good deeds or any traditions. Jesus said in John 14:6, *I am the way, the truth, and the life: no man cometh unto the Father, but by me.*"

"So, are you saying that being a good Amish girl and always obeying the church rules and keeping the Amish traditions has nothing to do with preparing me for Heaven?" she asked.

"Yes, that is what the Bible says according to the verse I gave you. There are many other Scriptures that verify it, and the Bible never contradicts itself," he added.

Immediately, thoughts of regret flashed through her mind - *was I foolish to ask cousin Rudy to destroy my harmonica? Was I not condemned for having it after all?*

"But what about the church rules, and what good…?"

The words had barely escaped Rosanna's lips when she heard the crunching of buggy wheels on gravel in the driveway behind the house.

When Clemens saw the panic on Rosanna's face, he immediately stepped away from the door to leave. He didn't want to cause trouble for her.

She hurriedly thanked him for coming and asked him to stop by again sometime.

Clemens waved goodbye and made a quick get-away!

As he drove out the front driveway, Rosanna walked around the corner of the house toward the back driveway. *A second unexpected visitor in one morning?*

Suddenly, anxiety struck her heart when she realized it was none other than Mem and two of her younger sisters. *Hopefully, Clemens drove away soon enough.*

"What a surprise! I didn't know you were coming over today," she remarked, struggling to remain calm. She sensed that Mem may have seen the car leave the front driveway.

Her sisters chatted excitedly about their visit to the Amish bulk food store over on Miller Road, almost five miles away.

"Did you find some good bargains at the store?" Rosanna asked nervously, trying to divert possible questions.

Mem told her about their purchases and the joy of having the pantry well stocked again. They walked past the garden toward the front door.

The sisters soon ran off to the big rope swing under the shade tree in the yard. It gave Mem the perfect opportunity to ask the dreaded question.

"So, who was in the car that just left?"

Rosanna cringed inwardly, but Mem continued talking without waiting for an answer.

"We had a visitor too this morning. That cousin of mine, Clemens, from California stopped by again. When I didn't answer the door, he went on his way. We don't need to hear his deceptive jargon."

Suddenly she paused, and her eyes widened as she glared at Rosanna. "It wasn't him that just left, was it?"

Rosanna blinked and lowered her eyes, then nervously reached down to pluck a weed out of the crack in the sidewalk. She realized an honest answer could ignite a wildfire of questions. She felt as if she was trying to find her way out of a dark room without doors! Since she would not lie, she had no choice but to face the inevitable.

"Yes, that was Clemens," she said. "But he didn't stay long. He was on his way to the furniture shop and needed directions," she said, shrugging her shoulders.

Alarmed, Mem erupted with an avalanche of questions.

"Why did he stop here? What did he talk about? Did he say anything about his religion? Or did he try to persuade you like he did me?"

But before Rosanna could respond, Mem continued.

"We don't want to give heed to his perspective on anything. Remember, he forsook the Amish faith and traditions. We must guard against being deceived by such people, or believing contrary to what our forefathers have taught us."

"Yes, Mem. We didn't visit very long. But, um... don't you agree he is knowledgeable in the Scriptures though?" she asked.

"That may be true, but it is important to learn how to interpret them correctly too."

Rosanna knew Dat would hear about it after Mem got home.

Her heart was heavy as she quickly peeled the potatoes and fried the chicken for lunch.

Chapter 7

Rosanna's mind drifted as she mashed the potatoes. She could imagine Dat's reaction to hearing of her run-in with Clemens. She groaned inwardly, wishing she had a reason to stay at David's house for the weekend.

Coming in from the fields at noon, David and Ben found relief from the blistering sun as they sat at the table. They hungrily devoured the chicken, potatoes, and vegetables which Rosanna had skillfully prepared for them.

She quietly forced down her own food as they chatted and joked in casual conversation, oblivious to her subdued spirit.

"Thanks for the feast, Rosanna!" David pushed his chair back. "Too bad you can't stay here longer and really fatten us up!" He chuckled, not realizing she would give almost anything for the chance to stick around for a few more days. But she gave him a forced smile and said, "You're welcome."

Rosanna was up early on Saturday morning. She had a few things to accomplish before she would go home that evening.

After breakfast she tidied up the kitchen, mopped the floors, and dusted the furniture. She did not expect that the spare bedroom would need cleaning since they rarely used it. But she opened the door to check anyway.

Surprised for a moment, she took a few steps towards the bed. Why were there several yards of folded dark green fabric laying there? She stepped closer -- a note!

"Rosanna, I don't need this extra fabric and I thought you might enjoy making a dress out of it, from Aunt Barbara," she read aloud.

She squealed with delight and was immediately in love with the color as she picked it up and admired it.

A glance at the clock told her it was only ten o'clock. *If I hurry, I could cut out all the pieces before lunch and finish it this afternoon. I won't be going home until later in the evening.*

Her Mem's teaching of using another dress as a pattern would come in handy now. But she wondered if Grandma's old sewing machine stored in the closet still worked.

At noon she wasted no time in telling her brothers about finding the treasure in the bedroom.

"Oh, yeah!" David said, sheepishly. "She dropped that off last week. Sorry, I forgot to give it to you."

"You're fortunate you didn't get a burnt lunch in revenge, big bro," she joked.

"Let me know if you need my supervision in making that dress," he teased. "Just remember, don't get too carried away if you want to show it off to Paul tomorrow night. Mem will demand to inspect it first, if she'll even allow you to wear green," he winked.

"Get out of here! I don't need yours, or anyone else's interference with this project, thank you!" she said, landing a playful punch on David's shoulder.

Rosanna soon had the machine dusted off and humming as she enjoyed the gratifying opportunity to sew unsupervised to her heart's content! However, she felt she was multitasking as her thoughts were also busy pondering over her future.

Since I have talked to Clemens again, how can I sit through another baptismal class tomorrow and pretend to be in agreement? she wondered.

The possibility of dropping out of class without causing much turmoil in her family and the church was far-fetched. She felt guilty even considering it.

The next day, Rosanna attended yet another baptismal class. With baptism day only two months away, she calculated they were almost halfway through the course of instructions. The thought of being forced into deciding soon nearly put her stomach in knots.

After coming home from church the rest of the family enjoyed their afternoon nap. *This is my chance to take a quiet and peaceful walk by myself!* She tucked a small New Testament into her dress pocket and quietly slipped out the back porch door. Glancing across the green pasture, looking for the perfect place to go, she decided to take the cow trail behind the barn. It led her along the pasture fence row down to the rippling creek in the woods.

When she reached the creek bank, she gathered up her long skirt tail as she comfortably positioned herself on a log beside the gentle flowing waters and kicked off her shoes. It was a perfectly peaceful and secluded haven! She drank in the beauty and serenity of her surroundings, God's creation. She longed to wash all her troubles down the stream and let the surrounding peace engulf her soul.

Once again, her daydreaming turned to the Scriptures which Clemens had shared with her. She reached for the little book in her pocket. *Maybe reading the passage again would help me comprehend it better in this place of beauty and tranquility.*

There it was - Ephesians 2:8-9, just like Clemens had said. "For by grace are ye saved through faith; and that not of yourselves: it is the gift of God: Not of works, lest any man should boast." She read it aloud. *It sounds liberating, yet almost unbelievable.*

The still small voice in her heart kept repeating, "*Clemens is right! The Bible says salvation is a gift.*"

"A gift"... "a gift"... It was as if an echo was sounding through the woods.

How does one receive the gift, as Clemens said? Just believe it? Can it be that simple? Isn't there anyone else besides Clemens who interprets it this way? My parents? My best friend, Emma? No one seems to understand. Is Clemens the one confused? Perhaps I am being deceived, she agonized, digging her toes into the sand under her bare feet.

I can't go on like this, I must know! Is there anyone who can help me? Her mind was spinning out of control! In her anguish and turmoil, she buried her face in her hands in an attempt to escape from it all.

Finally, she lifted her head and looked toward heaven. With tears streaming down her face, she cried out to God, "If it is that simple, God, help me believe it and repent of trying my way. Please, send someone who will stand with me and not condemn me for trusting and believing your Word, and your promises. I don't want to lose my family and all my friends, especially Paul," she prayed.

She soon rose to her feet, dried her face, and drank in one last view of the serene setting. As she watched the cool waters gently flow over the rocks, she realized her heart was lighter, as if God had washed at least some of her troubles down the stream. "Surely, God understands and knows my heart," she whispered, sensing His presence.

With renewed courage, she turned and headed back across the pasture and up the cow trail toward home with more life in her steps than she had all day.

She yearned to discuss her thoughts with Paul, but had feared being misunderstood and possibly jeopardizing their relationship. However, she resolved to let it be the evening she would conquer her fears and share her heart with him. She couldn't bear to keep it from him any longer. No matter the outcome, she had to face it!

She was nervous, yet eager to know his response to the burden on her heart. She prayed again for wisdom and God's guidance.

When she stepped into the kitchen, the pleasant aroma of their traditional Sunday evening dinner of chicken and dumplings greeted her. She felt a tinge of guilt for not helping prepare the meal, but she assumed since it was Sunday they would excuse her. *I had more important issues to deal with this afternoon.*

Soon everyone else around the table appeared to enjoy the multiple lively conversations, except Dat and Mem. They appeared downhearted and worried recently. Rosanna couldn't help but sense she was to blame for their solemn mood. She wished she could avoid hurting them.

When dinner was over, Rosanna hurried upstairs to change into her Sunday dress and brush back her hair before Paul arrived to take her to the youth singing, which would be held at the Mast's home this evening.

In a few minutes she heard her sister Laura call up stairs, "Rosanna, Paul is here!"

Rosanna grabbed her bonnet, hurried downstairs, and out to his buggy. As she put her foot on the steps and grabbed onto the side of the seat to pull herself up into his buggy, her foot slipped and she nearly fell to the ground. In embarrassment, she quickly brushed herself off, and tried again as Paul reached out to help her.

"Are you hurt?" he asked in alarm.

"No, I'm fine," she said, embarrassed that she had let her nervous self be so clumsy. She tried to calm herself, lest Paul would notice and ask questions. Now was not the time to discuss an important subject. They chit-chatted about the week's events.

CHAPTER 8

When they arrived at the Mast home, they joined the other youth in the large living room to sing the traditional German songs in unison. Rosanna found a seat beside Emma and quickly tried to catch up on the latest news before they announced the first song.

"Have you told Paul yet about what is troubling you?" Emma whispered to Rosanna.

"No, but tonight is the night," she responded. "I'm nervous and not sure just how to approach it."

Just then, Paul started the first song, and everyone else joined in. Rosanna loved hearing his deep, robust voice. Secretly, she felt bad for him, wondering if he'd be singing so happily if he realized what she had on her mind.

As soon as the singing ended, all of the guys who had a date rushed to get their horses hitched up to their buggies. One by one, they drove up to the front yard gate to pick up their girlfriend.

Paul was the second name called out, and Rosanna remembered to be careful getting into the buggy this time, even though she was still nervous and getting worse by the minute.

When they arrived at her home, Paul tied his horse to the hitching post. Together, they quietly entered the kitchen, being careful not to awaken the rest of the family as it was already ten-thirty. After getting a snack of cookies and a coke, they went into the living room to visit for the rest of the evening.

When they were seated Paul mentioned the beautiful dresser on the other side of the room, although he had often seen it before.

"I really enjoy my job working at the furniture shop, making beautiful pieces like that. It makes happy customers too. We even had a former-Amish customer from out west stop by recently. He was a rather unusual and interesting guy. We visited quite awhile, but it seemed all he wanted to talk about was the Bible. I must admit he was very knowledgeable and rather passionate about his beliefs. He also kept mentioning something about 'salvation,' and insisted it is important to know what it means."

Rosanna's jaw dropped as she listened, wide-eyed and spellbound!

Paul paused and replied, "Sorry, I didn't mean to alarm you or anything."

"No, I'm fine," she assured him. "Was his name Clemens, and does he live in California?"

"Yes, that sounds right," he said.

Rosanna lowered her gaze.

"But who told you?" he asked, astonished and perplexed.

Paul became even more baffled when Rosanna slowly lifted her head, blinking back the tears as she nervously began.

"Paul, I hardly know how to tell you this, but I had prayed for an opportunity to talk to you about this tonight. I'm rather overwhelmed by God's love in showing me He cares by guiding our conversation. From what you are telling me, I'm convinced it was my mem's cousin Clemens, who came to the shop."

"He is a relation to your mem?" Paul asked, wide-eyed and listening intently as she continued.

"Yes, and I have met him once and heard him talk about his beliefs twice. My life has never been the same since that. As you mentioned, he likes to talk about 'salvation.' My parents say his religion is full of false teachings, and I want to respect their opinion. But Clemens said we can not earn Heaven by our own merits. I've looked it up for myself in the Bible. It does say that salvation is a gift to all who trust in Him! Jesus paid the penalty for our sins."

Rosanna got up and took the plate with one remaining cookie to the kitchen, giving Paul time to respond.

"I understand why you are troubled, Rosanna. It's confusing, yet intriguing. But we're always cautioned to be on guard against false doctrines, or anything contrary to our traditions and beliefs."

"Right! I hear it in every baptismal class," she said, wearily.

"What would you think if I dropped out of baptismal class?" she blurted out before she'd talk herself out of asking him. "I don't have peace in making that commitment at this time."

"Clemens may have confused you, Rosanna. But remember, he obviously didn't keep his commitment to the Amish church. Maybe he is not the one to whom we should listen."

Rosanna lowered her eyes. She had hoped for at least an encouraging response.

"Your next class is still over a week away, so let's pray about this until next Sunday evening. I don't know what else to tell you."

Rosanna nodded, thankful that he planned to come back after such an unsettling date.

Soon, their allotted time was up at one o'clock. They said their goodbyes as Paul left with a promising smile!

Minutes later, Rosanna laid her head on her pillow and stared at the ceiling in the dark. Paul's remark, "Clemens may have confused you," kept her awake long past midnight.

Was Cousin Clemens deceiving me? Should I just try to dismiss what he said and move on with life as it used to be? But how could I do that? she wondered for the hundredth time. Her confused mind continued to drag her onto the bumpy roller coaster of skepticism.

Although relieved that their relationship was not in jeopardy so far, she realized her future could potentially have some difficult mountains to climb and deep valleys to cross if she continued going forward.

In the morning, the rooster crowed at the crack of dawn as always. She couldn't remember at what late hour she had last checked the time before drifting into a much-needed sleep. She only knew her body told her that the rooster crowed much too early.

Mem scurried around in the kitchen making sure the fried potatoes and eggs were ready when the rest of her crew came in from the barn.

As Rosanna set the table she sensed she was being watched. But she didn't mind, her groggy head was barely functioning well enough to carry on a sensible conversation.

"Did you sleep well?" Mem asked.

"Yes, after I finally fell asleep." She was glad Mem asked no more questions.

After breakfast Dat asked Rosanna to go to town to pick up some parts for the hay baler. As old Tony slowly trotted down the road, she had ample time to let her overloaded mind wander.

At last she pulled up behind the hardware store and tied Tony to the hitching pole.

As she entered the store through the front doors, an elderly employee named Mr. Walton immediately offered his help. She recognized him as the gentleman who occasionally drove the Amish into town for their doctor appointments. She asked for the baler part according to Dat's description. He retrieved it quickly from the next aisle and handed it to Rosanna. His expertise impressed her.

Carrying on a casual chit-chat for a few minutes, Mr. Walton asked, "Do all of your farmers use hand balers? Isn't that a lot of hard work?"

"Yes, traditionally, that's what the Amish use, and we're used to hard work," she said.

"Is it a religious thing? Why not use the more convenient methods available? Just curious," he said.

Rosanna squirmed inwardly, knowing her answer would make little sense to him.

"Our people farm with old-fashioned methods instead of following the ways of the world," she said, hoping her answer would satisfy him.

"Oh, I see! You believe we are the world?" Mr. Walton asked.

"Well, I don't want to offend you; but yes, that's what we believe," she responded.

"Do you mind if I share my interpretation of it?" he asked.

"No, go ahead!" she said, eager to know what he'd say.

"According to my Bible, the biblical definition of the world is people who have not repented and received God's gift of salvation. Are you familiar with that term?"

Just my luck to run into another 'gift guy,' flashed through Rosanna's mind.

"In fact, I have been told about it and read it, but it's hard for me to grasp the concept since it's contrary to what I've been taught. And what would you do if you weren't permitted to agree with such teachings?" she asked nervously, making sure no one else was within earshot. She hoped no other customers would come in and interrupt their interesting discussion.

"Aren't you free to choose what you want to believe?" he asked, surprised.

"No, we are not…" she paused, in search of a brief explanation.

"That's sad! The Bible states salvation is a gift, we can't earn Heaven. It's found in Ephesians 2:8 *For by grace are ye saved through faith; and that not of yourselves: it is the gift of God.* Other passages confirm that," he added.

"Yes, I've heard that before," she said.

"Good morning, Sir!" Mr. Walton turned his attention to greeting another customer coming through the door.

Rosanna quickly thanked Mr. Walton and hurried out the door. She untied Tony and urged him to speed up the pace as she turned onto the busy paved road. *I don't want to give an explanation to Dat what had kept me so long.*

During the drive home, she tried to process her discussion with Mr. Walton. *Perhaps God is in this!*

Nine

CHAPTER 9

On Wednesday morning, it was not a surprise to Rosanna to see neighbor Henry Mast enter their driveway. They immediately assumed the Mast's baby had arrived during the night.

Mem greeted him at the door and soon realized their assumptions were correct. He was there to pick up Rosanna to be their maid, which had been pre-arranged.

The baby was born at home, but when complications arose, they took the mother and baby to the hospital. Rosanna would care for the little children at their home while Henry stayed with his wife at the hospital for a few days.

Three sweet little shy faces and their grandmother greeted her when Rosanna arrived at their house. After she received the basic instructions, Rosanna was soon washing dishes, and tidying up the house after their grandmother left.

A couple days later, her heart skipped a beat when both of her parents came over in the afternoon. *What happened? Was something wrong?* Mem soon assured her there was no emergency. They just needed to talk to her.

After Dat had tied his horse to the fence post, he joined them in the living room. Mem sat on the hickory rocker with a solemn expression. Dat sat down in the other hickory rocker as he looked at Rosanna.

"Your mem and I decided we'd come over during these children's nap time so we can talk with you about some issues that seem to be troubling you."

Rosanna nodded. It was the moment she had been dreading for a while already, but she didn't expect it to happen at the neighbor's house. She respectfully sat on the couch with her hands in her lap trying to prepare herself for the inevitable and hoping to avoid too much conflict.

"Rosanna, it is my understanding that some things you've heard over the last year from Clemens about his religion have confused you. Is that correct?" he asked.

She lifted her eyes and looked at him. "Yes, I don't know what to think at times. But I believe he has some valid points and biblical knowledge which may be worth considering."

"But was he encouraging you to keep what we've taught you from your childhood?" He asked.

"No, but how can we say his teachings are wrong when he quotes it right out of the Bible? Haven't you always told me the Bible is true?" she reminded him.

"The Bible is always true, Rosanna. But we have to be careful not to misinterpret it. We must always remember if it is contrary to our church guidelines, and the traditions of our forefathers, it is most likely a false interpretation."

"What did Clemens say that troubles you so much?" asked Mem.

Rosanna lowered her eyes, not sure how to answer tactfully.

"Well, Clemens said, the Bible tells us we can not earn a home in Heaven since salvation is a gift. Jesus paid for our sins with His blood, death, and resurrection. He even gave Scriptures to prove it. But the preachers in class keep teaching us we need to do our best to please Him, which is our only hope of Heaven. There seems to be a contradiction.

"Are the preachers telling us the Truth, or is Clemens's interpretation wrong? They can't both be right. Who am I supposed to believe?" she said, throwing up her hands on the verge of tears.

"I also learned that the Bible says, in John 14:6, that Jesus is the only way to Heaven," she added, while being careful not to mention who told her about that.

"I'm sorry you are so confused, but as we've always tried to teach you; believing in Jesus is evidenced by a lifelong obedience to Him. We believe that includes abiding in the traditions and regulations of the Amish church," added Mem.

"Getting baptized and joining the church should help clarify things for you over time," said Dat.

"Well…" Rosanna shuffled her feet. "I don't know how to say this, but I'm not sure that I want to get baptized this summer. I don't have peace about it yet."

Dat's jaw dropped, and Mem gasped in disbelief. *What had their own daughter just said?*

"How could you even think of refusing baptism?" Mem asked as she teared up.

It was not the path she had envisioned for any of their children. How could they ever endure the disgrace and humiliation of a disobedient child? She wondered.

Dat quietly hung his head in deep disappointment. He had never expected this from their tenderhearted Rosanna.

At last, he lifted his head and stood to his feet, indicating to Mem it was time to go home.

Then he turned to Rosanna with the saddest eyes she'd ever seen in him and said, "I hope you'll consider the consequences before you make any rash decisions.

"Ultimately, it's your choice to make; but remember, some day you'll answer to God for the decisions you make. And I must inform Bishop Yoder about this too," he said.

Other than saying goodbye, they slowly walked out the door in awkward silence.

Rosanna watched them through the window until they were in the buggy and had gone up the road. Only then had she turned around, dropped onto the couch and wept. It pained her to see her parents so deeply grieved.

I don't mean to be a rebel. But what am I to do?

Shortly, the little ones woke from their naps and helped lighten her heavy heart. She entertained them until it was chore time. Little Reuben, Linda, and Susie toddled alongside, excited to help feed the chickens and the baby calves in the barn. There was only one cow to milk.

After finishing up outside, she let them watch her prepare a light dinner to be ready when Henry would come home to be with the children for the night.

When the dishes were washed and everyone had tired of playing games, she helped Henry prepare the children for bed. He tucked them in and retired to his room.

At last, Rosanna climbed the stairs to her room and dropped into bed emotionally exhausted. She wondered what surprise twists life would throw at her tomorrow aside from Henry bringing his wife and baby home from the hospital a day early.

Soon it was Saturday evening, and Rosanna was glad to be back home to sleep in her own bed. She knew the following day was a day of rest since it was not their bi-weekly church Sunday. She was also anticipating an interesting date with Paul after the singing. *He will be surprised by my run-in with another religious guy who told me the same thing that Clemens says about the gift!*

Arriving at her home after the youth singing on Sunday night, Rosanna and Paul sat on the porch swing enjoying the cool evening breeze brushing softly across their faces. Their conversation soon turned to the subject weighing heavily on both their hearts all week. Rosanna cautiously related her unexpected run-in with Mr. Walton at the hardware store to Paul. She was unprepared for his surprising response!

"Rosanna, I must admit I did more Bible studying this past week than I've done in a long time. What I discovered was very intriguing! I had never before heard or understood some of the things I found when searching more deeply and carefully comparing the 'gift' Scriptures with other Scriptures.

"I even asked my dat about a few of my findings. He couldn't deny it either since it was right there in the Bible. But he still cautioned me to be vigilant since we can misinterpret the Bible."

"So do you think Clemens and Mr. Walton are right?" she asked, hoping for some answers.

"Well, I believe they are onto some Truth, but I don't see that it excuses their lifestyle," he said.

"My parents would agree with you on that point. They are opposed to any unfamiliar Bible teachings and are grieved about my interest in Clemens's view of Scriptures. However, I have little time left to decide if I want to commit to the church membership or decide not to join this summer," Rosanna reminded Paul.

CHAPTER 10

Almost two weeks later, soon after dinner on a Saturday evening, Rosanna had glanced out the kitchen window just in time to see a buggy come in their driveway. Her heart skipped a beat or two as she quickly recognized Bishop Yoder and Preacher Sam climbing out of the buggy. She assumed her dat was expecting them as he came out of the barn and met them at the hitching post.

Rosanna wanted to escape out the back door. It was too late! Mem had already seen her peer out the window and came to look for herself. Obviously, it was no surprise to her that the bishop had come to visit.

Knowing that the nature of their visit would not be suitable for the youngsters to hear, Mem hustled them all upstairs before the callers entered. She told the children good night and instructed them to play games or read until bedtime.

Rosanna forced a smile to greet Bishop Yoder and Preacher Sam as they entered the living room. Dat offered them a seat as Mem sat on a chair next to him.

Realizing she caused the meeting, Rosanna wanted to sit as far off to the side as she dared. It seemed the room crackled with tension as she braced herself for the inevitable.

After a few minutes of casual chit-chat, Bishop Yoder turned his attention to Rosanna. He cleared his throat before diving right into the issue at hand.

"Rosanna, I'm glad you joined the baptismal class this summer. Do you feel you are ready and willing to join the church with the rest of the class in several weeks from now?"

For a long frightening moment, all eyes turned upon her awaiting her reply. She fixed her eyes on her fidgeting hands in her lap.

How could I possibly tell them how I feel? My honest answer could be perilous, no matter how I present it. With her legs shaking and heart thumping, she seized the moment. *It's now or never.*

At last, she lifted her eyes and glanced at the bishop. "I must tell you, I don't have peace about getting baptized and becoming a church member. It seems some teachings I hear in our class contradict what I read in the Bible," she said relieved she had the bravery to voice her opinion.

"Rosanna, I can assure you, we would never wish to teach you anything other than the Truths from the Bible," said Bishop Yoder. "Our forefathers have worked diligently to establish the right path for us to follow according to their interpretation of the Scriptures. We can uphold our church guidelines and traditions with confidence. We have a heritage that we ought never take for granted," he reminded her.

"I have always been taught the Bible is the Word of God. But do you believe there could be some fallacies, especially when it contradicts our rules and traditions?" she asked.

Bishop Yoder shuffled his feet nervously. "No, I believe the Bible is always reliable, but sometimes certain points of doctrine can be misinterpreted by people seeking to follow their own ways. As I've said before, we need to uphold the teachings and examples our forefathers left for us to follow," he explained.

"And I think we'd be wise not to doubt our ancestors who studied diligently to interpret the Bible to the best of their understanding," he added as her parents and Preacher Sam nodded in agreement.

An hour of futile discussions from either side only intensified Rosanna's frustration.

At last, when Rosanna did not indicate a change of heart, Bishop Yoder glanced at the clock and decided it was getting late. He looked at Preacher Sam and asked if he had any additional advice for Rosanna.

"Yes, I would also like to remind you, Rosanna, that you are very privileged to be born into an Amish family. You have parents who teach you the right way, and I'd encourage you to follow in their footsteps," said Preacher Sam as he rose to leave.

Rosanna didn't feel obligated to respond as Dat followed the men out the door. She was relieved when the door closed behind them. It was not a good evening from her perspective.

Bishop Yoder had also informed her they would not allow her to continue with normal social privileges if she didn't follow through with baptism. She choked back tears as she analyzed the bishop's verdict.

Rosanna looked at her mem still sitting in her chair drying her eyes. The thought of her daughter possibly dropping out of the baptismal class was unacceptable. She could have imagined it of the wild Chris Troyer, but not of her own daughter.

Rosanna agonized between the guilt of ruining the "perfect family" reputation and a desire to obey her conscience concerning biblical Truth.

When Dat returned to the living room a few minutes later, he reminded Rosanna that it was not too late to continue with the baptism plans.

"I'd regret seeing you having to break up your relationship with Paul," he said.

"What do you mean, Dat?" Rosanna gasped.

"Do I have to be a church member to date Paul from now on, even though I wasn't a member when we started dating?" she asked in disbelief.

Dat nodded, "That's what Bishop Yoder decided would be best. Since Paul is a church member, he should not be in a relationship with one who is old enough to be a member, but refuses to join. Such a one is obviously not in good standing with the church," he added.

Rosanna sat speechless. *How much harder can life be when seeking to make biblical choices?*

At last, she told her parents' good night and headed toward the upstairs.

"Rosanna," her mem spoke softly.

She hesitated at the bottom of the stairs and responded, "Yes, Mem?"

"Your dat and I will pray that you'll change your mind and do what is right. We tried to teach you the right path. But you have to choose if you want to be right with God, or take your own way and bring dishonor upon our family," she said tearfully.

Rosanna nodded and softly climbed the stairs to her room as she tried to avoid waking her siblings.

She wept into her pillow as she lay in bed, mentally re-living the evening. *I can not bear the thought of losing Paul. How could I ever break the terrible news to him? Furthermore, I had never meant to cause my parents such grief and disappointment,* she groaned silently.

Laura stirred next to her in bed. *Oh no!* She didn't want Laura to wake up and wonder why she was in such distress. She was relieved when Laura continued snoring.

Rosanna thought again of Bishop Yoder's explanation in response to her questioning of the "gift of salvation."

"Since Jesus knew we would fail, He died on the cross to forgive our sins. Salvation is a free gift to us if He deems we've done our best to please Him," Bishop Yoder had struggled to clarify.

She realized his explanation did not match up with Clemens's and Mr. Walton's interpretation of the Bible.

Finally, when Rosanna realized it must already be the wee hours of Sunday morning, she tried to calm her mind and get a few hours of sleep before breakfast.

Several hours later, sitting at the breakfast table, she was thankful it was not their church Sunday with another baptismal class to attend. She needed time to sort out her scrambled thoughts from the previous evening.

That evening, as Paul and Rosanna returned from the youth singing, he wasted no time asking how her week had turned out.

She told him about Bishop Yoder's and Preacher Sam's visit the previous evening. Then, lowering her eyes, she said, "And we won't be allowed to continue our relationship unless I follow through with baptism and become a member in good standing with the church."

She lifted her head as Paul took her hands in his. With concern, he gazed into her tearful eyes for a long moment. Then he whispered softly, "I will never let them take you away from me!"

Her heart fluttered as she smiled, "Thanks!"

"Rosanna, I have spent a lot of time studying my Bible in the last few weeks, and I see where you're coming from. I think you may be correct in some of what you've learned from Clemens and Mr. Walton," said Paul.

She smiled and squeezed his hand, delighted to hear him say that!

Finally, someone willing to stand with me, rather than condemn me. God answered another prayer! If only my family and Emma would understand me too.

"I don't know where our future is taking us," Paul continued. "But I will support the decision you feel prompted to make concerning baptism. I wouldn't want to force you into deciding against your conscience. God can safeguard our relationship as He pleases."

"Thanks for your patience and understanding, Paul," she smiled. "Let's pray about it every day."

On the following Wednesday, Rosanna and Laura went to David's rental farm to harvest some produce in the garden they had grown for him.

They enjoyed working together, not only as sisters but also as friends. Laura was aware that not all was peaceful in Rosanna's life. She wished to understand what was troubling her sister to warrant a visit from the bishop.

"Laura," Rosanna said as she paused from her work. "I don't wish to make life complicated for you, but I've learned some things about our Amish traditions and beliefs that apparently are contrary to the Bible."

Laura leaned on her shovel and stared at Rosanna, clueless. *Had her sister gone crazy?*

"What are you talking about? Aren't you getting baptized and becoming a church member in a few weeks?"

"Well, it's difficult for me to become a church member and commit to observing the rules, and help strengthen the church when I don't agree with their teachings," Rosanna explained.

"What kind of teachings? Are you hearing something unusual in class?" asked Laura.

"No, of course not. But you wouldn't have heard of it anyway since you're not a member yet. It's just that someone has shown me some Scripture passages that are hard to ignore."

Laura frowned, "Where did you get these ideas? Don't you remember the warnings we always hear about not giving heed to false teachers? The devil goes around *like a roaring lion, seeking whom he may devour*, the Bible says. Must've been a loud roar!"

"Oh, I didn't realize you can preach so eloquently," Rosanna chuckled, throwing a small potato at Laura which she had just dug out of the ground. Laura dodged just in time to avoid getting thumped on her arm.

"And I didn't realize you're such a poor aim," Laura teased right back.

"Now, do you still want me to tell you what I was talking about?" asked Rosanna.

"Yes, but don't make it very confusing," Laura winked as she grabbed a bucket to pick the tomatoes. *What was really going on between Rosanna and her parents and Bishop Yoder?* she wondered.

Eleven
CHAPTER 11

"That sounds strange! No wonder the bishop came over to talk to you!" Laura exclaimed loudly just as David walked past the garden on his way to fetch a tool from the workshop.

"What is so strange, and what did you do, Rosanna, to alarm the bishop? If I may ask," David said, hesitating at the garden gate.

Rosanna had not noticed David passing through, but now she felt obligated to explain Laura's remark, even though he was eavesdropping.

"Well, I have some doubts about my baptism and committing to church membership this summer."

David's jaw dropped! "What! Why?" he asked in disbelief as he listened wide-eyed.

"Well, it all started when Mem's cousin Clemens visited us a while back. She tried to shield us from him, but I overheard him quote something from the Bible that has puzzled me ever since. However, I'm not sure you want to hear it since your life might never be the same," she cautioned him.

She wrapped her long dress around her legs as she reached for a bucket, and squatting down, began picking green beans in silence.

After David found his voice again, he said, "Well you have me curious now, so you might as well give me the rest of the story."

"Well, if you insist," she teased.

"Clemens said we can not gain Heaven by our lifestyle, or even by doing our best. Eternal life is a gift. Jesus paid the price on the cross for the forgiveness of our sins. We must repent and put our trust in Him alone to receive His gift. He said it means no man enters Heaven except through Jesus."

Rosanna paused, waiting for David's delayed reaction.

"Yes, I see what Laura was saying," David answered. "It does sound strange, and even dangerous. It's not what we are taught. What do Mem and Dat think of it?"

"They are grieved and strongly opposed to such teachings, as you would expect," she said soberly. "And they wouldn't appreciate me repeating it to you and Laura either. But you asked!" she added.

"Well, I wouldn't take it too seriously, coming from Clemens. He apparently enjoys the ways of the world, so I imagine he'd say whatever justifies his lifestyle. We need to be careful and not be deceived by false teachings," David reminded his sisters. Laura nodded in agreement as David turned to leave.

"Oh yeah," he turned back to Rosanna. "Think twice before you drop out of baptism now, if you want to have a part in my wedding this fall. You know how that works. Besides, don't get yourself in so much trouble that you'll put your relationship with Paul in jeopardy too. I'm just warning you, as your big brother," he said before continuing on his way.

Rosanna had hoped for some degree of understanding from David. But then she couldn't blame him either. He had his mind on a bright and exciting life ahead with his future wife, Miriam.

Several long hours later, Rosanna and Laura had finished gathering the produce and carried it to the enclosed porch. They made plans to come back later to process it in jars to store in the basement for the winter food supply.

It was time to hitch Tony to the buggy and head home. Dat would need them to help with the evening chores.

On much of the way home, Laura was softly humming a melody, while Rosanna agonized over making a monumental decision by Sunday concerning baptism. She was rudely awakened from her daydreaming when Tony turned into their driveway. He knew he was home.

She watched the free-spirited Laura bounce from the buggy. *Oh, to be carefree again!*

She dragged her own body off the seat and climbed out. *Heavy decisions and burdens have a way of exhausting even young people like me.*

On Friday morning, Rosanna was on another errand in town. She hurried to pick up the sugar, butter, and baking powder in the grocery store. *But where was the cooking oil?*

She turned at the end of the aisle a bit too fast and almost ran into an elderly gentleman. She apologized politely for not paying attention before hurrying to the next aisle.

"Oh, hi!" the elderly gentleman was speaking to her.

She glanced at him quickly, then did a double-take. "Mr. Walton! Sorry, I didn't notice it's you!" she exclaimed.

"It's okay. I saw you were quite intent on shopping. You must have a lot going on, being in such a hurry!" he chuckled. "I've been thinking about our brief conversation in the store a while back. Were you able to read your Bible concerning the things I mentioned to you?" he asked with genuine interest and concern.

"Yes, and I need to make a major decision before Sunday morning. Maybe you can give me some advice," she said timidly.

She immediately sensed a prick of her conscience, asking an "outsider" for advice in church matters, especially concerning baptism. She knew her parents would not appreciate that.

"How can I help," he asked calmly.

Rosanna nervously glanced up and down the aisle. Then she lowered her voice. "Well, I've learned that we can't earn eternal life through our lifestyle or good deeds. Now I don't have peace about getting baptized and joining the church. I'd be required to promise obedience to the church regulations and support our Amish lifestyle. Wouldn't that make me a hypocrite?"

"What are the consequences if you choose to opt out?" Mr. Walton asked.

"Well, I'll have less social privileges, and I'd have to break up the relationship with my boyfriend among other things. We can't have an Amish wedding unless we both are members of an Amish church," she said.

"Oh, that must be a tough decision, Rosanna!" Mr. Walton exclaimed. "But ultimately, it's a choice you have to make between you and God. Everybody will stand before God someday and give an account for themselves. No one else can do that for you. Whether you accept His forgiveness and trust Jesus Christ only for eternal life will make all the difference."

Rosanna nodded thoughtfully. She knew he was right. "Thank you, Mr. Walton, for your encouragement. I have much to think about before Sunday. But I better hurry before someone comes searching for me."

CHAPTER 12

Oh, my leg! My leg! Rosanna groaned in pain as she lay in the roadside ditch along the dusty graveled Peachtree Road. She had been daydreaming on her way home from shopping and was oblivious to her surroundings. That ended abruptly when a barking dog came rushing out from someone's home to attack Tony.

In a daze, she realized the blood on her dress was coming from an ugly gash on her arm. But her leg was the source of the extreme pain she was experiencing.

She tried sitting up to determine her exact location. Then she saw that Tony's kicking spree and terrified get-away had ended a short distance away. He stood tangled in the fence along the road with the splintered remains of the buggy still attached to him. She was thrown out when her rig plunged down the steep embankment.

Rosanna looked at her leg again and realized she had never before seen it bent at such a strange angle. She moaned in pain as she tried to move. Reaching for her apron, she pressed it hard against her arm to slow the bleeding. She worried about how long she would be there until someone would come along and find her along the normally quiet country road.

A quick prayer had barely escaped her lips when she heard a vehicle come to a screeching halt on the road above her. She was touched that God had immediately answered her prayer!

Rosanna couldn't have been more thankful to see her neighbor Gary come rushing towards her.

"Are you hurt? Are you ok?" he asked repeatedly as he scrambled down the steep embankment to her side. After a quick observation of her injuries, he hastily jerked his phone out of his pocket and called his wife Joyce at home.

Although Gary lived only five minutes from the accident, it seemed like half an hour until Joyce came speeding down the road. She brought Dat and Mem with her.

When her concerned parents examined her injuries, her broken leg appeared to be the most urgent, requiring attention immediately. Gary offered to call the ambulance, but Dat and Mem hesitated to incur more bills than necessary and therefore declined the offer.

They soon had Rosanna carefully lifted into Joyce's car and lying down on the back seat. Joyce, accompanied by Mem, sped off to the hospital twenty-five miles away. Gary and Dat followed shortly thereafter in the truck.

In the meantime, Levi and Laura came to untangle Tony from the fence. They would lead him behind their buggy the rest of the way home, but first they gathered up the groceries scattered in the ditch. Dat would come after the wrecked buggy the next day.

At the hospital, Rosanna groaned in pain as her broken leg was set and wrapped in a heavy cast. She was thankful it did not require surgery. After her arm was stitched up, it was not long before she was released to go home.

When Joyce brought her home, Dat and Gary carried her into the house. The doctor at the hospital had instructed her she needed to keep her leg elevated for several weeks. After getting comfortable on the living room couch, Gary and Joyce prayed with her and left. Their kind prayer deeply moved Rosanna.

At last, she was able to calm down and reality engulfed her. She realized God had temporarily taken care of her pressing decision concerning baptism. In her present condition, she wouldn't be able to attend church for a couple months. Baptism day would have to happen without her presence.

She did not wish to be laid up, but she felt relieved that God intervened on her behalf. Paul was the only one who knew her secret perspective of the accident when he came to see her later that evening.They both recognized God's hand at work in her circumstance.

Meanwhile, Dat and Mem's hopes were dashed. They had prayed for Rosanna's commitment to the church and their traditions. It would help her unsettled heart, they assumed. Having no choice except to give her another year to decide about baptism was worrisome, especially to Mem.

At last, two weeks after the accident, it was baptism day. A wave of mixed emotions flooded Rosanna's heart as the rest of the family left for church. Her younger sister Martha stayed home with her. She was a good caregiver, bringing her a glass of water and re-adjusting the pillow under her injured leg.

"There! That should feel better. I'm sorry you can't be with the rest of your class on baptism day. It must be a great disappointment to you." Martha tried to think of more ways to comfort Rosanna's heart.

"Thanks! I will be fine. God has allowed this to happen, and I must trust He makes no mistakes," Rosanna assured her. Her pretense of regret slightly pricked her conscience. However, Martha was clueless.

Rosanna reached for the Bible on her bedside stand. It was her source of comfort in times of trouble. Psalm 46:1, *God is our refuge and strength, a very present help in trouble.*

When her Bible fell open to the book of Psalms, she turned to her favorite passage, chapter twenty-three.

"My Shepherd!" She immediately recalled Mr. Walton's explanation of this at the hardware store. He had said, "Not everyone is entitled to say, *The LORD is my Shepherd.* Although He died for everyone, only those who receive Him by faith are His sheep. His saving grace is available and sufficient for all. But it is effective only for those who repent and put their trust in Him alone for eternal life."

Rosanna realized that unless Jesus is her personal Shepherd, then the rest of the Psalm does not belong to her. She remembered again why this is one of her favorite chapters in the Bible. *The Lord is my Shepherd, I need not worry.*

She closed her Bible and laid her head back on her pillow. *Truly, my cup runneth over!*

She sensed that God would use her healing time to grow her in His Word and prepare her for an extraordinary future. *My Shepherd will lead the way.*

After a few minutes, her mind wandered to the church service going on at the Beachy's home. They were probably in the process of baptism at the moment. She thanked the Lord for intervening. Otherwise, she either would have been one of them, or she would have been in significant trouble all around.

Martha, curled up on the hickory rocker, glanced at the clock. She'd have time to read a few more chapters in her novel before it was time to prepare a quick lunch for Rosanna and herself.

Rosanna wished the clock would speed up just for a day. She looked forward to her Sunday afternoon visit with Paul. He would update her on all the details of the day. She would not even have to fake regrets for being absent. *He knows my heart,* she thought drowsily as she began to doze.

What was all the clatter and noise? Being awakened from her afternoon nap, Rosanna became aware that her family was home from church. The quiet time had ended.

Mem came to check on her and chat for a while about the service. "It saddened my heart to see your empty place on the baptismal bench. But God allowed your accident to take place. We don't know why, but He does," she said. Rosanna couldn't have agreed more.

At the first chance she had, Rosanna privately asked Laura about the baptism. "How did it go?"

"Mem looked sad all day," Laura answered. "She and Dat are still hoping you'll be able to join next spring, but I'm sure they're concerned about your lack of commitment to our Amish faith."

"I'm sorry to cause them such grief and heartache. I don't mean to dishonor them or to be disrespectful," Rosanna said, truly sorry to inflict pain on her parents' hearts.

"But according to the Bible, Laura," she continued. "I am held accountable to God for what I have learned. Romans 14:12 says, *So then every one of us shall give account of himself to God.*

"Only faith in Christ will get me to Heaven, not Amish faith. Amish faith is just that -- faith in Amish traditions and rules rather than in Christ. Jesus said in John 10:9, *I am the door: by me if any man enter in, he shall be saved...*" Rosanna nearly startled herself with her own boldness and confidence in proclaiming these newly discovered Truths. She was grateful that the Bible verses she had been meditating on had come to her mind so readily.

"Saved?" Laura wrinkled her brow. "What does that mean? Sounds like you're getting your nose rather deep into the Bible. Don't suffocate the things they have taught you," she warned half sarcastically.

Rosanna rolled her eyes, "I think you're trying to be funny, but it is an important matter."

"Popcorn!" Mem called out from the kitchen. Their favorite Sunday afternoon snack was sending its delicious aroma through the house. Rosanna was delighted that Paul arrived just then and was able to enjoy some popcorn with her.

Thirteen

CHAPTER 13

That fall on a clear October day, David grasped Miriam's hand. "Can you believe our wedding day is only a week away?" he asked excitedly.

Her face beamed at the thought of it! But she also realized that it was much easier to count down the days than count off the things on their to-do list.

Everyone was running on high energy, making certain the house is entirely spotless. The new dresses, women's *koppa* (plural for *kopp*), men's shirts and suits all had to be made on the sewing machine and neatly pressed.

Most of the last week had been spent preparing a variety of foods for the wedding feast. They appreciated the help of the ladies who came to process chickens, bake dozens of cakes and pies, and prepare various other dishes. Rosanna enjoyed helping with these wedding preparations. Especially since she was now released from the heavy leg cast which had weighed her down for a few months.

Her heart also felt lighter since the agonizing decision concerning baptism became postponed. She would have until next spring to finalize her decision. A sigh of relief escaped her lips. She could expect less conflict concerning church issues for a few months. However, Rosanna had no doubt that she would still be under scrutiny by her parents and church leaders until spring.

On the wedding day, the large kitchen was soon buzzing with a flurry of activities, and the aroma of delicious foods was in the air. Paul and Rosanna had been assigned to help wait on tables together. Rosanna was thrilled to work side by side with her best friend!

Despite the busyness, Mem was disturbed all day about Rosanna's *kopp*! It looked fancier than normal. So did the other girls' *koppa* for the special occasion, she thought. But again, Mem wanted her daughter to set the example. Instead, she blended in with her friends more than usual, which Mem suspected was Rosanna's goal. She chided herself for failing to examine Rosanna's *kopp* before the wedding day.

Rosanna sensed her mem's watchful eye. No doubt a discussion would await her the next day. She was glad she was not a church member yet. The Bishop would not need to get involved.

Traditionally, their church perceived a honeymoon trip as a worldly custom. Therefore, a few days after the wedding it was moving day for the newlyweds. Since they had a minimal amount of possessions, they didn't need the usual neighborly help. With the help of their family, all their belongings fit neatly on Dat's all-purpose spring wagon for the eight mile trek to their beautiful little country farmhouse.

It was a long and difficult winter for Rosanna. Her relationship with Paul was her one bright spot in life. No one else understood her heart like Paul.

In the months following David and Miriam's wedding, Paul and Rosanna continued studying the Bible together on their weekly dates. Answers to Rosanna's forbidden questions began to surface. However, they agreed to keep their findings a secret as long as possible. That dreadful day of disclosure would come soon enough.

* * * *

Spring had arrived at last and with it came Dat's reminder, "The new baptismal class is starting next month."

Mem nodded, "I'm glad your leg has healed up now, so you don't have to miss out again."

Rosanna shifted in her chair. She was glad her younger siblings had already moved away from the dinner table and were out of earshot. For a moment, she feared her courage would fail, but she braced herself. "I don't know how to tell you this, and I'm sorry to let you down. But I'm not comfortable getting baptized and joining the church this summer," she stammered.

Mem's eyes welled up with tears as Dat simply stared at Rosanna in disbelief. *It can't be happening,* they thought. *Our daughter still refusing to follow in our footsteps is inconceivable! Where have we gone wrong?* they agonized. This was definitely not the expected results of striving for the perfect family they had envisioned.

Dat eventually found his voice again. "Rosanna, we've tried to teach you the path of righteousness. Don't you appreciate your godly heritage? Why would you not desire to continue in our Amish faith, our hope of Heaven?" he asked with great concern and disappointment in his voice.

Rosanna was glad he asked, as it gave her the opportunity to explain it once again. She abruptly went into the living room and returned with a Bible from the bookshelf. She opened it to her favorite verses.

"I don't have all the answers, but I believe the Bible tells us we get to Heaven through Jesus Christ alone." She began reading in John 14:6, "*I am the way the Truth and the Life, no man comes unto the Father but by me.* According to that, I can not earn eternal life by my lifestyle or church membership.

"Dat, Ephesians 2:8-9 says, *For by grace are ye saved through faith; and that not of yourselves: it is the gift of God. Not of works, lest any man should boast.* It seems this is saying that I cannot make myself righteous and eternal life is a gift through Jesus. Am I misunderstanding these Scriptures?" she asked.

Dat lowered his gaze. After a long moment, he looked at Rosanna. "You need to remember that our ministers preach the Bible as our forefathers understood it. They deemed any other interpretation to be a false doctrine. We cannot be like Clemens and live as we please, then boastfully say we know we are going to Heaven. We must do our best to please Him. Then, Rosanna," Dat concluded, "it is for God to decide our destiny on judgement day."

Mem nodded again in agreement as she wiped the tears running down her cheeks.

Rosanna's desire was not to argue with her parents. Yet, she felt compelled to tell them more. "There is no room for boasting since it's not any of my own work, Dat. Jesus paid my sin debt in full." She read it again, "*Not of works, lest any man should boast.*"

"It's not always what it sounds like when reading the Scriptures, Rosanna, but it is important to understand it accurately. Sounds like you've been listening to the wrong people, one of which is Clemens. We won't allow him to visit here anymore if I can help it," Dat said with determination.

Rosanna cringed. That was not what she had hoped to hear.

Dat paused momentarily. Then, shaking his head, he pushed his chair back and left the table.

"Rosanna, you know there will be serious consequences if you continue down this destructive path. Our entire family will suffer from your errant ways," Mem said in a worried tone.

Rosanna watched as she slowly walked into the living room. Sadness gripped her heart as she realized that she had inflicted inevitable pain upon her own parents. *Lord, give me strength to do the right thing,* she prayed silently.

Laura had almost finished washing the dishes when Rosanna got up and offered to help her.

Her sister was silent and confused as they worked together. She had overheard the entire conversation, and her heart pained for both her parents and Rosanna. She sensed their peaceful family closeness was being torn apart by grievous disagreements and heartaches. *What will happen next?* she wondered. Laura wished to make it all go away, and for life to return to normal again.

When Rosanna could stand it no longer, she broke the woeful silence. "Laura, are you enjoying the book you borrowed from Aunt Barbara?"

It drew Laura back to the present. "Yes, it's an interesting book," she stated simply.

"Can I read it after you're finished with it?" Rosanna asked.

Laura nodded, "Yes."

Rosanna realized her sister was not in a talkative mood. Neither was she. They quietly finished up their chores in the kitchen and retired to their rooms until bedtime.

Fourteen
CHAPTER 14

Every morning for the next few weeks, the moment Rosanna woke up, her thoughts turned to another distressing day ahead. She thought of her grief-stricken parents aimlessly going about their daily duties with shoulders slumped. Her siblings often tried to avoid the tense atmosphere in the house by staying busy outside.

She knew everyone rightfully laid the blame right on her shoulders for tearing up their family bond; a painful burden she must bear.

Had I never known Clemens or Mr. Walton, my family would still be enjoying a life of apparent peace and happiness! However, those thoughts quickly lost their stronghold when she remembered it was God's hand that was obviously at work in her life.

God had allowed her "accidental" hearing of the Gospel through Clemens, thus causing her to be intrigued by it. He had answered prayers and also brought Mr. Walton across her path. God intervened in her decision concerning baptism last summer. He gave her courage and peace to decline baptism and church membership in the spring. Thus, she could trust Him to continue leading the way. Her eternal destiny was at stake, she reminded herself.

A month had gone by since Rosanna had informed her parents of her final decision regarding baptism. Their church became aware of her decision on the first Sunday of new baptismal classes when Rosanna was not among the candidates. Everyone sat in silent disbelief, but the gossip soon raced through the community like a wildfire about the "rebel" of the "perfect family."

Dat and Mem sought counsel from Bishop Yoder multiple times concerning the disgraceful situation. He echoed their concerns of Rosanna's harmful influence on her siblings. His advice was gut-wrenching, but they agreed to heed it for the sake of the family.

It came as no surprise one evening at bedtime when Dat asked Rosanna to wait in the living room while all her siblings went to bed. She had no doubt why she was asked to wait. Oh, how she dreaded it! *Lord, help me!*

Mem looked sadder than ever, and Dat didn't hesitate to get right to the grievances on their minds. "Rosanna, we are concerned about your errant ways, and your influence on the rest of our family. It causes us to believe it's best to ask you not to speak to others about your unacceptable views of the Bible. We wish it wouldn't have to be this way.

Dat paused momentarily as if trying to delay some dreaded news. "If you can respect our request, we'll allow you to remain at home. We'll give you some time to reconsider our wishes and your upbringing. In the meantime, think about the dire consequences of your choices. Rejection of your training is sure to take you down a dark path of remorse. Remember, a day of reaping what you have sown is coming."

When Dat finished speaking, Rosanna sat speechless. *Remain at home? Was Dat serious? Where else would I live? Would they really ask me to move out?*

Yes, she remembered. *Dat is always a man of his word. But perhaps this one time, grief influenced him to make a decision which he would regret later and recant.*

She could barely whisper goodnight as they dismissed her to go upstairs. Dropping into bed, she felt her breath being suctioned right out of her lungs. Her shattered heart cried out to God as she wept.

Never in her worst nightmare could she have imagined the crushing pain. She expected her parents' to reject her stance. Yet her heart pained beyond words at the reality of not being welcome in her own home. *I really am an outcast!*

The threat of being severed from her family and close friends was more than she could humanly bear. *What about Paul? Would they take him away too?* She agonized and prayed fervently for God's grace to help face the daunting future.

Sunday evening could hardly come soon enough for Rosanna. In the privacy of the living room, she was finally able to update Paul on the most recent turmoil in their home.

"I realize it's all my fault. I don't want to break up our relationship, but what can I do? Unless I keep silent about my new faith, they will not allow us to continue dating, nor can I live at home anymore. And, you know me, I can't keep quiet. But I have nowhere to turn," she said misty eyed.

He studied her face for a moment. His heart was moved as her beautiful blue eyes reflected the pain in her sincere heart and soul. "Rosanna," he began gently, "I don't doubt that God has opened your eyes and heart to understand His word the way you do. You are an adult, responsible to follow Him wherever He leads. He has also revealed more Truths to me recently, and I understand what you mean about disagreeing with the church's teachings.

"God may have a plan for us that we can't even imagine today! They may force us to separate for a season, which will be rough. But, as I've said before, I'm certain God can bring us back together in His timing. So don't lose heart."

Rosanna wanted to laugh and cry simultaneously! Her love for him and his understanding nearly caused her heart to burst!

By the time Paul left, they had made plans for Rosanna to contact the Waltons somehow. Possibly, they would give her a temporary home, and Paul would find a way to keep in touch.

Parting was painfully difficult for them that evening. They didn't know where or when they would meet up again.

The next morning Rosanna somehow performed her normal kitchen duties, although her mind was far from it. She discovered there were only a few cups of flour left in the pantry when Mem asked her to bake a batch of bread for the week.

"Well, evidently someone needs to make a run to the bulk food store this morning. I suppose it will be you. Everyone else is already occupied with their assigned duties for the day," Mem said.

"I'll go," Rosanna offered.

The next moment Dat popped in the door. Striding to the desk in the corner of the living room, he retrieved his checkbook to pay the feed salesman who had just dropped off a load of feed for the cattle.

Mem informed him of their need for a few groceries. "Rosanna is available to go if you want to harness Tony for her."

Dat eyed Rosanna warily. Mem read his mind and informed him she'd only be going over to the country bulk food store.

"I'll have Tony ready to hitch to the buggy whenever you're ready to go," he said as he glanced at Rosanna.

"Thanks," she said, reaching for her bonnet as Dat hurried out the door to the waiting salesman.

Mem quickly had a short grocery list prepared. "I'll try to be back shortly," Rosanna called over her shoulder as she headed out the door.

"Be careful," came Mem's motherly reminder.

Tony didn't seem particularly enthused about getting hitched to the buggy again. However, Rosanna urged him along. She wanted to impress Mem with her quick trip! She covered the three miles to the store in good time.

Tony snorted as she tied him to the hitching rail next to another Amish customer's rig. Rosanna noticed a few cars parked along the side of the driveway, which was not unusual. Non-Amish customers also frequently enjoyed shopping at the unique country store.

When Rosanna stepped inside, an Amish employee greeted her with a friendly welcome. Making her way down the middle aisle to the baking supplies, she heard a lively conversation in the next aisle. The one voice sounded familiar! They were not speaking Dutch. She paused… *What! It couldn't be him!* She grabbed her groceries and hurried around the corner to confirm her suspicion.

She gasped, "Mr. Walton!"

His friend moved on, and Mr. Walton turned toward her. Rosanna tried to swallow the lump in her throat. Again, she knew their surprise meeting was not an accident.

Mr. Walton's face lit up, eager to visit. After a few minutes, Rosanna lowered her voice, "I need to talk to you. I desperately need your help!"

His eyes widened, "What's wrong? Are you in danger?"

Rosanna shook her head, "No."

Glancing at other shoppers down the aisle, Rosanna spoke softly again. "I must hurry, but can you meet me down the road at Miller's corner? I can't let anyone see me talking to you very long in here," she said.

"Sure! I'll wait for you at the corner," Mr. Walton assured her.

As Rosanna paid for her items, the Amish cashier threw uneasy glances at her, the "community rebel!"

Rosanna hurriedly loaded her groceries into the buggy, untied Tony, and hastened down the gravel road. Mr.

Walton was already waiting at Miller's corner. There was no house in sight, and a grove of trees provided additional privacy.

Mr. Walton stepped out of his car and swiftly walked over to her buggy. "What is going on?" he inquired anxiously.

Rosanna nervously glanced down the road. Nobody was in sight, but that could suddenly change.

"To give you a quick overview of my dilemma…" Rosanna began hurriedly, "this spring when the new baptismal class started up I decided not to join. It's devastating to my parents and the community. I told them how I had come to that decision. Now, my parents have forbidden me to discuss my view of the Bible with anyone else if I want to live with my family. Honestly, I can not agree to be quiet. So, moving out is my only option. But, of course, no Amish will take me in."

Was that a tear glistening in the corner of his eye as he listened?

The kindhearted, white-haired saint gave none other than a typical godly and compassionate response, as she had expected. "Rosanna, I want you to know our doors are always open to you! We have a spare bedroom. My wife, Darlene, and I would be delighted to let you stay with us as long as you need a place. Hopefully, your family will recant soon."

"You can't imagine what your kindness means to me," Rosanna replied, "although I certainly don't want to be a burden on anyone."

"We're more than happy to be a help to you. Let us know if you need help moving your belongings," said Mr. Walton.

"Thank you so much! I must hurry home now, but I will be in touch with you this week," she smiled.

"Sure," Mr. Walton said, getting back into his vehicle as Rosanna picked up the horse's reins. She watched as his car disappeared around the curve in the road ahead. She could only imagine what it would be like to get around that fast.

Arriving home, Rosanna entered the kitchen and dropped the groceries on the table. Mem was busy at the sewing machine in the living room. Rosanna was thankful she did not ask why it took longer than usual to get the groceries.

As she got started mixing the bread dough by hand, Rosanna's mind was racing. *I had not planned to sneak away, but it might help me to avoid a dramatic departure. How can I secretly contact the Waltons to pick me up later this week?* She wondered. So far, it looked rather impossible. She recognized her desperate need for God's intervention again.

On Wednesday morning when an egg customer knocked on the door, Mem asked Rosanna to take care of the lady's order. She took her customer to the basement where the eggs were kept cool. During their friendly chat Rosanna was astonished to learn that Mr. Walton was her uncle.

She immediately recognized the opportunity to contact the Waltons and requested a favor from her customer. The kind lady willingly agreed to be her messenger. Rosanna quickly scribbled a note on a piece of scrap paper, hoping neither Mem nor her sisters would come to the basement just then. Her hands were shaking as she nervously folded it and found a small piece of tape to secure it. She sent the note with the customer to the Waltons, asking them to pick her up at home on Friday evening after dark if possible.

Fifteen
CHAPTER 15

Rosanna's spirit soared! *God did the impossible again! I believe He is with me!* She was convinced only God could have so perfectly arranged for her parents and younger siblings to be away when the Waltons came to pick her up on Friday evening. He spared her from the heart-wrenching scene of her parents' grieving her departure. Only Laura and her brothers were at home with her that evening.

Rosanna had her bag packed, expecting the Waltons any minute. She glanced around her room. *When will I ever see this place again?*

Then, before her heart would fail her, she grabbed her big duffle bag full of clothing, her Bible, and ran downstairs.

Poor Laura! She would have to break the grim news to Dat and Mem that someone worldly helped her sister leave to who knows where?

As Rosanna hugged her sister goodbye, her own heart was breaking to see Laura weeping. She was the only family witness since the boys were still in the barn. They were unaware of her plans to leave.

"I'll be back to visit sometime if Dat and Mem will let me come," she tried to comfort Laura.

"Please do! I'll miss you terribly," Laura wept.

"I'll really miss you too, Laura!" Rosanna said as she turned and went out the door before she would break down in front of Laura. She felt like a wretched sister, yet at peace with God.

The Waltons were waiting in the driveway. Knowing her parents might show up any minute, they loaded her things swiftly and drove away.

Laura was glad it was dark. She couldn't bear to see them drive away with her sister and best friend. She sobbed broken-heartedly, not knowing when she would ever see her again.

The Waltons turned left and were just going up the road when they noticed lights coming over the hill behind them. Sure enough, the car turned in at her home. It had to be her parents. Rosanna thanked the Lord for His perfect timing. Yet, she couldn't help but envision the scene at home in the next few minutes.

Her brothers come in from the barn and discover what had happened. Laura informing the rest of the family. The weeping, the mourning, the utter despair resembling the death of a family member!

Suddenly, the thoughts, *how could you do such a disgraceful thing to them,* and *I had no right alternative* were waging an intense mental battle in her reeling mind. *How could something feel so wrong, yet seem so right simultaneously?* She couldn't explain it.

She prayed for strength, remembering God's promises. *The Lord is my strength and my shield…* Psalm 28:7.

Arriving at the Waltons, she didn't know what to expect. But she was about to experience a life in complete contrast to her upbringing. They served her a bedtime snack as they sat in the living room to visit.

At bedtime, Darlene showed her around the house before leading her down the hallway at the opposite end of the house from the living room. "Welcome to your new home," Darlene smiled as she introduced her to a beautifully decorated bedroom, a modern bathroom, and even a spacious closet. "Let me know if you need anything," she said before joining her husband again in the living room.

"Thank you, I appreciate your kindness and generosity so much," Rosanna said. She was awestruck as she glanced around her room apprehensively. *The beautiful dresser. Fancy curtains and soft colorful bedding. The fluffy carpeted floor! Family pictures on the wall.* Everything was so foreign to her. She even had a bathroom to herself, with a stash of bright fluffy towels. *How does anyone sleep in such an elaborate environment?*

Morning came bright and early, just like back home. But something was very different. Everything was quiet with no one stirring. Was she the only one awake? She tried to get a few more minutes of rest. But her anxious mind wouldn't calm down, racing back to her home. *My family would already be up and finishing up the morning chores. A steaming breakfast would be on the table! But my chair beside Laura's is empty.* Suddenly, all the sad faces around the family table flashed before her eyes. She rolled over, trying to bury the mental image under her pillow.

I can't allow myself to dwell on that, she promptly scolded herself. *The Lord is my strength!*

Thirty minutes later she heard the Waltons moving around in the kitchen. *What were all the strange noises and beeping sounds?*

Rosanna slowly threw back her light covers and stepped onto the fluffy carpet. She stood for a moment gazing at her long dark dresses in the closet.

They looked strangely out of place. *I doubt I'll be wearing those the rest of my life.*

Where is my life headed? So many uncertainties in her future. She thought of the song lyrics she read in school years ago, "One Day at a Time…"

* * * *

Rosanna was glad to stay "at home" the first few weeks and work for Darlene. Being out in public would be risky until she became more established in her new environment. The natural step for her parents to take would be to locate her and try to convince her to come back home. She did not look forward to that first confrontation.

However, with each passing day, she found her mind drifting back to her family more frequently. She dearly missed them, especially her siblings. After three weeks, she finally asked the Waltons to take her back home for a visit on a Sunday afternoon.

Rosanna's stomach tightened as they approached the family farm.

Dat and the younger siblings came out to the car to see who their visitors could be. His mouth dropped open when he realized it was his long-lost daughter. Immediately, his eyes glistened with tears!

Rosanna struggled to keep her composure.

"Hi Dat," she said cautiously.

"Hello, are you coming in?" He asked hesitantly.

The Waltons wisely waited in the car while Rosanna followed the rest into the house.

Nothing had changed on the outside. But inside the house did not feel the same.

Upon entering, Rosanna noticed that Mem was not in the kitchen like usual.

Neither was she in the living room.

"Where's Mem?" She ventured to ask Dat.

"Mem has not been feeling well ever since you left. She spends a lot of the time in bed." He motioned toward their bedroom.

Walking into the bedroom, she heard sniffles. Rosanna resisted turning and running out the door. She forced herself to sit on the side of the bed, attempting to visit as Mem sat up in bed.

"We miss you so terribly, Rosanna! I beg you to change your mind and come back home! You know your leaving has brought disgrace upon our family name! It can't be pleasing to God. I've not been well, thinking about you so much." She dabbed her eyes with her hankie.

Rosanna bit her lip, fighting back her own tears. "I'm sorry you're feeling ill, Mem," she said softly. "And I'm sorry to disappoint you so, but it would be wrong for me to deny the Truths God has shown me, all for the sake of traditions. It doesn't mean I love you any less, I will always love you. But I must do what is right for the sake of Christ. I'd gladly explain it again."

"No!" Mem covered her face with her hands, shaking her head. After a brief moment she said, "We thought there would be no greater honor than for all our children to become loyal Amish church members. But now that joy has turned to shameful sorrow.

"If our forefather's knowledge of the Bible was adequate for them, it ought to be sufficient for us as well. We have never found, nor sought, anything better," Mem continued.

Rosanna sensed that a short visit would be best. "I don't want to keep the driver waiting too long, so I need to go, Mem. I hope you feel better soon, and I'll pray for you!"

"There is one more thing I need to say before you leave, Rosanna," Mem stopped her. "Please, whatever you do, I pray you won't change your way of dress to look like the rest of the worldly people out there. Oh, I can't bear the thought of it!"

Rosanna listened respectfully, then told her mem good-bye and headed toward the front door.

Dat paused in the kitchen and said, "You know we want you back. You are welcome here whenever you change direction and return to what we've taught you from your childhood." His face was etched in pain as he spoke.

Rosanna could not find an appropriate response, so she followed him out the door in silence.

Will all future visits always be like this?

Sixteen

CHAPTER 16

One early summer day on a Monday evening, six weeks after Rosanna had left home, there was a gentle knock on the Waltons' front door.

Rosanna scurried off to her room. She listened intently, hoping it wasn't someone coming to demand that she return to her family.

Mr. Walton welcomed the visitor in and she could hear Darlene laughing and offering the visitor a seat. Rosanna strained to hear more. She gasped, and suddenly her heart was racing! *I know that voice!*

She was out of her room and down the hall in a flash! Entering the living room, her suspicions proved to be true!

"Hi, Paul! I can't believe you're here!" she exclaimed, beaming and grinning from ear to ear.

"Good evening, Rosanna! Yes, can you believe I was brave enough to come?" Paul responded excitedly. It seemed they had not seen each other since forever.

Mr. Walton kindly offered them seats in the den where they could visit in privacy. They both had much catching up to do. During a pause in the conversation, Paul asked, "How do you feel wearing a store-bought dress? It makes you look even more beautiful!"

"Thanks!" Rosanna felt her face blush slightly. "I'm growing more comfortable every day with my new clothes. It is incredibly liberating to choose the styles and colors I want to wear! I don't even have to buy the fabric and make it myself anymore!" She chuckled, remembering her early teenage sewing frustrations.

"I'm free in Christ, and no longer in bondage to man-made rules! The Holy Spirit is now my guide," she said happily.

"How are your parents coping with your view of things by now?" Paul asked her, guessing he already knew the answer.

"Not well. Mem is refusing to accept it so far. I keep praying for her," Rosanna answered.

"I talked to Emma at the youth singing on Sunday night. She sorely misses you and wants to see you. Obviously, her parents won't allow that," Paul informed her.

After a moment, he added, "Oh yeah, your cousin Rudy began dating her recently."

"Oh, I'm so happy for both of them!" exclaimed Rosanna. "Did you tell her you were coming here tonight?"

"No," he whispered, "this is our secret. I just couldn't stay away any longer, no matter the cost! I've missed you tremendously! Do you think the Waltons will tell anyone?"

"Not if we ask them to keep it confidential," she answered. "They are such sweet and godly people! You can not imagine what a blessing and encouragement they've been to me.

"They take me to church every Sunday which I enjoy so much. The Pastor studies for his sermons and preaches from his notes alongside the Bible. It's all so new to me. I can't seem to get enough of his interesting preaching," Rosanna explained excitedly.

"I'm thankful to see you enjoying church again and seeing you so happy and enthusiastic about life! Your lovely eyes sparkle again!" he said with a sweet smile.

"Yes, God is good to me! I want to keep growing in my walk with Him," Rosanna beamed.

The evening slipped away quickly, and before they knew it, Paul's driver was back to take him home. They were not ready to say goodbye again.

"I will see you again soon," Paul promised her. "My parents won't be home from their trip to Ohio visiting my ailing grandparents until next week. So being home alone gives me the opportunity to slip into town whenever I can," he winked with a chuckle.

It was rather late when he arrived home and crawled into bed. Closing his eyes, he mentally rehearsed the secret and encouraging visit. His heart was overflowing with love and admiration for his persistent and courageous girlfriend. She had a peace which he could not yet fully grasp.

Suddenly, the longing for true peace and happiness welled up in him like the thirst of one lost in the desert.

Moments later, as he envisioned the rough path required to reach that peace and happiness, fear unexpectedly gained an ugly grip on him. A still voice pierced the heavy darkness around him, *Are you willing to make the sacrifice she has made to receive the peace she has?*

He groaned, rolled over, and closed his eyes again. It was too much for his tired brain. He willed himself to fall asleep.

Paul's surprise visit that evening carried both of them through the week until Friday night. He went back to see her again before his parents would return on Monday. They knew only God could make a way where there was none for them to meet again in the following weeks and months. How they prayed!

Rosanna's visits to the home farm became fewer and further apart as fall approached. Although she longed to stay in touch with her family, she dreaded the confrontation on every visit. She missed the fun interaction with her siblings. *How I wish for just one peaceful visit with them!* Her love and burden for them kept taking her back to see them again and again.

The Amish religious system would not allow them to treat her as family. She understood that, but she resolved to keep the door of communication open as long as possible. It was her only hope of sharing her faith with them. Obviously, they were not willing to receive anything from her viewpoint yet, but she prayed daily that the time would eventually come when they would.

* * * *

One chilly morning that fall, the Waltons dropped Rosanna off at the dentist's office.

Upon entering, she quickly scanned the waiting room. She gasped! *What!* Paul also had a Dentist appointment that morning? She was not sure which one of them was more surprised!

She immediately realized God had answered another prayer! They moved to a quieter area of the office as they tried to catch up on the latest family news. There was no chance of anyone eavesdropping on their German dialect.

Their conversation soon turned to more serious matters. Feeling confident they wanted to spend their future together, they couldn't help but realize it looked bleak and difficult to achieve. *What did God have in mind?* It was a question they asked themselves almost daily.

Paul would not think of asking Rosanna to recant and return to bondage, as she referred to the Amish religion. She'd have to become a church member to get married, and joining the church was not an option in her mind.

Together, they considered the sacrifices required of Paul if he also left the Amish church and they were to get married.

His parents were depending on him and his future wife to care for them and the farm in their golden years. His nieces and nephews all looked up to him, their hero! Additionally, his grandparents would evidently depart from this earth soon. And they would leave a significant inheritance for each grandchild of the Amish faith. So far, their family circle was still complete and encased in the Amish religion. However, Paul knew all these things would not hold a candle to Rosanna and her obvious peace and freedom.

Their visit ended abruptly when the dental assistant called out his name. He quickly assured her they'll meet again soon and disappeared down the hallway.

Rosanna absentmindedly browsed through a newspaper that had been laying on the little table as she mentally processed their conversation. It would grieve Paul's parents if he also became a prodigal for her sake. She cringed to think of causing more broken hearts.

At last, it was time for her appointment and they called her name. She dreaded the noise of dentist tools and equipment, but she found comfort in thinking perhaps Paul was in the room next to her!

Seventeen
CHAPTER 17

As autumn turned into winter, Paul slowly, but surely made progress on the rugged path toward his future which stretched out before him into the vast unknown. God's leading was evident, but his heart was anguished.

"Why must families be torn apart as a result of following biblical teaching? It's not the brotherly love that the Bible speaks of repeatedly," he lamented to Rosanna during one of his evening visits.

She empathized with him, having walked the difficult path to freedom herself - the lonely life of a "rebel" who broke the secure Amish family circle of religion; the rejected "orphan" seeking a place to call home; the loss of close friendships; the difficulties of adapting to a new culture and lifestyle. Rosanna had learned those were only a few of the deep ruts and speed bumps on the road to freedom and peace with God.

As Paul continued his pursuit of peace with God he soon realized that without the strength of God and the Holy Spirit's guidance, his complicated journey would lead to a disaster. *...without me ye can do nothing,* John 15:5.

A few months later, soon after New Year's Day, Paul took the courage to break free from the bondage of Amish man-made rules and traditions. When he told his parents about his decision, they were deeply grieved and disappointed. Yet, they were not entirely surprised, knowing he had his heart set on Rosanna.

"You could try to seek out a new relationship with a girl in our community," they pleaded.

"As much as I love and admire Rosanna, there is another matter of greater importance to me which inspired me to make the decision to leave. That is accepting the biblical plan of salvation and having peace with God," he explained.

After numerous scriptural debates with family and friends, he realized his words were falling on unregenerate hearts and deaf ears. Obviously, they perceived it to be the words of a heretic.

Paul expected to experience many of the same consequences that Rosanna had faced. Unfortunately, he was right, although his parents' and the church's reaction had not been as severe as he had imagined. The bishop in his district was slightly more tolerant than some others in the community and was criticized occasionally for being too lenient. However, he believed Paul's decision to leave was definitely cause for excommunication from the church.

Severed friendships and family rejections were heart wrenching for Paul. But he determined to set his eyes upon his Savior and never turn back.

He soon left all he had ever known and moved to an apartment in the town where Rosanna and the Waltons lived, thus starting a new life.

A few weeks later, he approached Mr. Walton for advice. "Do you have any suggestions where to find a job!? My bank account is not looking too healthy right now, and paying rent for my little apartment is draining it rather fast. I also need to buy a car." *It felt strange to talk about buying a car!* He thought. "I may need your advice on that too," he grinned.

"I understand," Mr Walton chuckled. "The Riverside Lumber Yard is hiring. How about submitting an application there?" He suggested.

"Sounds like a good idea!" Paul agreed. "I could even walk to work from my apartment until I can afford a car."

That afternoon, Paul went to the lumber yard to apply for work. A few days later he started his first day of work in modern society. His manager, Ryan, patiently allowed him much grace as he adjusted to the new culture.

His life appeared to be running smoother every day until a month later when Ryan asked to see him in his office. Paul couldn't imagine what he had done wrong.

In the office, when Ryan nervously cleared his throat, Paul feared it was not good news.

"Paul," Ryan began, "I appreciate your strong work ethic. You've been a dependable, hard worker at this place in the short time I've known you. However, we've had a few complaints - some of our Amish customers seem to have a problem with your presence here."

Ryan was quickly relieved when Paul's slight smile indicated he immediately understood the situation.

The objections did not come as a surprise to Paul. He had often seen Amish customers come in who left again almost immediately when they noticed him. He knew doing business with a former Amish church member was strictly forbidden by their church leaders.

Ryan continued, "I don't want to lose you as my employee unless you don't feel comfortable here. I'd like to promote you to an office position if you want to stay. The choice is yours. I would assign the other employees to deal with the customers."

"I-I'd like to stay if it's all right with you," Paul stammered, dumbfounded.

"Excellent! We'll get you trained for the office in the next few weeks," Ryan promised.

"Thanks for understanding and looking out for me, Sir!" Paul said gratefully as the short meeting ended.

Promotion! How fortunate can one be? Paul wondered. *God has taken what was meant for evil and turned it into a blessing!* He could hardly wait to tell Rosanna about this one! He hurried home after work.

Calling Rosanna instead of waiting to see her was still fascinating to him. He dialed her number… "Rosanna! Rosanna!"

"Yes? Are you okay? What's wrong?" she asked, alarmed.

"Yes! I'm fine," he assured her. "But you won't believe what happened at work today!"

Before she could respond, he blurted out, "I got promoted! How much better can it get? God is so amazing!"

"Wow! Praise the Lord! I'm so happy for you! I was going to call you after work, but in your excitement you beat me to it," she giggled.

"Oh yeah? Did you have something you wanted to tell me?" he asked, still trying to catch his breath.

"Well, the Waltons were taking me for an evening visit out to the farm again tonight. I have not seen my family in several months. I'd love to have you go with us and be my bodyguard," she laughed. Paul couldn't refuse the offer to ride along and agreed to go.

"I will not wear my Amish dress this time. I hope they will let me in," Rosanna explained.

"All right, so I need not wear my suspenders either?" he chuckled.

The sun was setting when the Waltons pulled up to Paul's apartment. He hopped into the back seat beside Rosanna. He wasted no time in telling the Waltons about his promotion at work.

The Waltons rejoiced with him. "When you live in God's will, you can trust Him to bless you and supply your needs. God is always faithful to His own," they encouraged him.

Fifteen minutes later Mr. Walton announced, "Here we are," as he turned into the driveway at the farm.

Laura and her siblings greeted them with friendly smiles. But Dat's smile faded immediately when he saw Rosanna's clothes. Turning his eyes toward Paul, he scanned him from head to toe also before shaking his head in disappointment. However, he surprised Paul when he quietly motioned them toward the house.

"Where is Mem?" Rosanna asked.

"Mrs. Yoder has not been well, so Mem went to visit her this afternoon. But she should be back soon," Laura answered.

After some tense and awkwardly casual chit-chat in the living room, they heard a buggy coming in the driveway.

"Oh, Mem is home," Laura commented as her siblings ran out the door to greet her. Laura followed shortly.

When Laura returned five minutes later, she glanced at Rosanna with sadness. "Mem isn't coming in until you leave. She doesn't want to see you 'spiritually disfigured' in those clothes, she says."

Paul and Rosanna exchanged glances and rose to their feet, making their way toward the door.

Dat cleared his throat. "It would be best if you two wouldn't visit in this way again. You may stop by if you wear your Amish clothes."

Resisting the temptation to refute his request, they walked toward the Waltons' car.

Rosanna turned to wave goodbye and winked at Laura who returned a smile, lifting Rosanna's spirit. She felt somewhat connected to her sister again. She missed Laura's sisterly friendship more than she had realized. How she wanted to bring Laura home with her!

Mr. Walton offered to take them to visit Paul's parents too. He had not seen them since he had left. But

Paul would wait until another day. One dose of rejection and stress was enough for the evening.

Sensing the somber mood on the way home, the Waltons perceived the evening had not gone as they had hoped. As they dropped off Paul at his apartment, they reminded him that they were praying for him and his family.

It was almost bedtime when they arrived home. Darlene offered Rosanna a snack, but she kindly refused and said, "No thanks, I'm really not hungry. If you'll excuse me, I'll just go right to bed."

Rosanna went to her room and closed the door behind her. Sitting on her bed, she thought over the happenings of the evening - *My own mem refused to see me! I should have expected it, yet it's even more painful than I anticipated.*

After changing into her night clothes, she slipped under the blankets. The hurt and tension of the evening slowly gave way to prayer. Prayers for strength and for her family, especially her mem.

She realized she may not be the only one having trouble falling asleep that night. She envisioned her mem's broken heart keeping her awake as well.

Rosanna prayed quietly in the darkness, "Lord, do what I cannot do - open my parents' eyes to your Truths."

CHAPTER 18

The month of May proved to be even more adventurous than the previous few months for Paul.

Passing his driving test with flying colors, and later buying his first car confirmed that he was no longer under the bondage and control of man-made rules. His only restriction was his bank account! There were no rules concerning the model, color, or style of the car! He knew a bright red car could be a source of pride, but so could a shiny new black buggy. *Not the color, but the heart matters to God*, he reminded himself.

A week after acquiring his cherished vehicle, Paul took Rosanna and her new photographer friend, Emily, on a trip to a surprise destination. Rosanna had never been treated to a more thoughtful birthday celebration!

He beamed with joy to have found a scenic mountainous park setting, complete with picturesque waterfalls. It was perfect for picnicking, hiking, and relaxing.

After a picnic lunch of her favorite foods and treats, they climbed up the incline to the waterfalls. Emily sat on a huge rock next to the water as Paul and Rosanna searched for just the right background to take their first professional photos together.

At last, they had found the perfect spot - a waterfall background with beautiful wildflowers strewn among the big rocks on a grassy knoll. Rosanna watched innocently, wondering why so much effort was made for birthday pictures? She had not known Paul to be such a perfectionist.

Just when she thought they were perfectly situated, Paul said, "Oh yeah! Let me hold one of these gifts for the picture!" Stepping aside, he picked up one of the smaller gift boxes that Emily had neatly arranged among the rocks for them to use as photo props.

Rosanna looked at the camera, ready for the first shot. *This is so romantic!*

Then, she suddenly realized Paul was no longer looking at the camera. He was on one knee, looking up at her, and grinning from ear to ear! "Rosanna, will you marry me?"

His love-stricken brown eyes locked with her sparkling blue eyes! Rosanna was never more surprised in her life! Once she recovered from the initial shock, she beamed and sweetly answered, "Yes. Yes, I will!"

Standing to his feet, He took the diamond ring from the "gift box" he held and slipped it onto her finger. "I love you!" he whispered sweetly, as they embraced.

She could not stop admiring her glittering ring as Paul gently brushed a tear from her cheek with his hankie. She had never felt so special and blessed in all her life! "God has demonstrated to us that He can do what had seemed impossible in our eyes a year ago," Rosanna beamed.

"Yes, God is gracious!" Paul agreed. He was bursting with pride and gratitude for his beautiful and godly fiancé!

The wedding would be another challenge in their new culture. But the Waltons had already proven themselves to be an invaluable source of guidance and encouragement to both Paul and Rosanna. They were overjoyed to see the couple advancing in their new environment.

In her joy and excitement, Rosanna temporarily ignored the nagging thought of having to tell their parents of their upcoming wedding. It would not be a cheerful announcement to their families since they would not be allowed to attend a non-Amish wedding.

* * * *

The summer was filled with many details that would lead up to their September ninth wedding day.

In August, while taking an Amish family on a shopping trip, the Waltons learned that Rosanna's cousin Rudy and her former best friend, Emma, were also getting married in September.

Rosanna knew Emma would also have regrets that they could not share in each other's special day. Another childhood dream gone awry. Instead, joyous new dreams were developing.

Rosanna had promised Paul she would get her driver's license before they got married. She was excited, yet getting behind the wheel proved to be more intimidating than she had envisioned. In a few weeks she would not need to ask Mrs. Walton to take her places anymore. She had climbed another rung in her ladder of freedom.

Three weeks before their wedding day, Paul and Rosanna could no longer postpone the dreaded trip. Although there was not even a slim probability that they would attend, their parents deserved to be invited to their wedding. Having been forbidden to bring their vehicle onto the farm, they asked the Waltons to take them once again.

Rosanna was glad to see Mem back in the kitchen again. However, after hearing of their engagement, the kitchen was filled with silence.

"Our daughter - having a fancy and worldly wedding! What a disgrace!" Mem muttered. "You know we can't come," she said as she turned away tearfully.

"Yes, we're sorry, but we understand," Rosanna replied regretfully.

They exchanged a few more bits of news and information, but Rosanna soon realized heading back to the car would be a wise idea.

Laura caught up with them at the yard gate and quickly informed them Clemens had stopped by to see them last week. But Dat had refused to visit with him and asked him to never come back. "'You've caused enough grief in our family,' Dat told Clemens," she said. Rosanna stared at her in disbelief.

"Laura, never forget what I've told you about the things Clemens taught me," she said. Laura nodded, and they hurried toward the car to keep Laura out of trouble.

"That didn't take long. I take it they were not thrilled with your exciting news," Darlene remarked.

"You're right," Rosanna replied, trying to contain her emotions. "They did not congratulate us at all. I'm sure they were looking forward to their first daughter's wedding. Their absence will sadden us too."

The ride home was mostly in silence. As they expected, it would not be a pleasant evening to remember. *Surely, there will be brighter days ahead*, they encouraged themselves.

On a Saturday morning two weeks before the wedding, Rosanna stood in front of the kitchen sink staring out the window. Absorbed in daydreaming, she had not heard Paul enter the Waltons front door.

"What do you see out there?" Rosanna jumped and turned away from the kitchen window at the sound of Paul's voice.

She tried to hide her threatening tears as she quickly remarked, "Oh! Sorry, I guess I was daydreaming again."

"I assume they were sweet dreams," he teased.

"To be honest, I was just imagining both of our families' involvement in our wedding, and how much we will miss having them enjoy this time with us," she answered him quietly.

His compassionate eyes looked into hers. "Yes, I know what you mean. And it makes my heart ache that your dat won't be here to walk my beautiful bride down the aisle to the altar."

"How will we make it through our wedding day without our families being present? If only I could hear my mem even once say, 'I'm happy for you!'" Rosanna said.

Instances such as this came more frequently as the wedding date drew near. Trying to hold each other up emotionally was a challenge at times. They had to remind themselves continually of Psalm 118:14, *The LORD is my strength and song...* They were reminded of God's faithfulness and mercy as their church family walked beside them to encourage and help them grow in the Lord. Rosanna's bridal shower hosted by the church ladies was a special blessing and encouragement to the couple.

Nineteen
CHAPTER 19

September arrived quickly, and along with it came Paul and Rosanna's wedding day. They were blessed with a beautiful day to be united in holy matrimony and to be pronounced husband and wife!

"What therefore God hath joined together, let not man put asunder," the preacher quoted.

What a sweet day it was, despite the missing loved ones! They marveled again at God's goodness in bringing them together. They were firmly convinced nothing is too hard for God.

After a brief honeymoon in the Rocky Mountains of Colorado, it didn't take long to move Rosanna's few belongings into Paul's apartment. Living in love helped turn their tiny apartment into a king's palace! Their hearts were overflowing with blessings from their faithful heavenly Father!

Over the following weeks, married life gradually settled into a daily routine as Paul continued to work at the lumber yard, and Rosanna continued with her position at the Daycare just down the street. Her mem had given Rosanna valuable hands-on training in child care. She looked forward to having her own children to train and care for someday.

It was early October when the Waltons picked up on a hot topic of the Amish community while taking several of their people to various doctor appointments.

It saddened Paul and Rosanna when the Waltons told them of Dat and Mem's plans to move their family several hours away to northern Indiana in a few weeks. They knew it was the typical reaction to the disgrace of their rebel daughter weighing too heavily on their minds. Perhaps a fresh start in a new community would blot out the stigma attached to their family name.

It surprised Rosanna, yet she rejoiced to hear that they chose a community with less conservative church regulations. She imagined her siblings would have more freedom to enjoy life in Indiana. *Should I dare hope that their spiritual perspective could also change over time?* she wondered.

Her thoughts turned to her brother David and Miriam and their new baby, Marvin. *How would they cope with them being so far away?* Her family would especially miss seeing their first little grandson and nephew grow up close by. However, she smiled at the thought of possibly seeing David and Miriam more often herself, since they would have no other family around.

Rosanna strongly desired to go out to the farm one more time before her family abandoned her childhood home.

A few days later, when Paul and Rosanna arrived on the farm, the family was relatively friendly, but in the flurry of sorting and packing, they had little time to stop and visit. Even Paul's car sitting in the driveway seemed to be ignored. *Were they just too busy to notice it, or did it not matter since they were moving anyway?* Paul wondered.

Paul and Rosanna wisely kept the visit short. After the goodbyes and wishing them well in their new home, it was time to leave. Her siblings continued to wave at them as they drove out of the driveway. Hot tears trickled down Rosanna's cheeks as she waved back to them. She glanced around quickly, surveying the old homestead one more time. How she would miss the farm! She realized their move was most likely her fault, yet she had no regrets for making the right choice, though forbidden. No doubt, life would go on.

Strangely enough, she looked forward to going to visit her parents and siblings after they got settled into their new home in Indiana. Within the month, Rosanna sent them a letter by mail to announce their plans to visit them on the day after Thanksgiving Day.

For the next couple weeks, she couldn't help but wonder, what their first visit would be like. *Will yet another attempt to break down the walls of separation bring us any closer to family unity? Will we be welcomed more than before? Will it be a worthwhile trip?* She was eager to find out if anything had changed after the sudden move to Indiana.

At last, it was Thanksgiving Day! They enjoyed a traditional holiday feast at the Waltons house, which was next best to a gathering with her own family.

The next morning, with a sense of apprehension, they began their journey to Indiana. They spent much of their time singing, praying, and preparing their own hearts to face whatever the outcome of their trip would be.

They arrived right after lunch while the family was still together in the house. Dat stepped out on the porch to greet them. He looked hesitantly at their car sitting in the driveway. Paul held his breath, hoping it would not close the door on their visit before it even began, but to his relief, Dat slowly turned to open the door and invited them inside.

Stepping into the kitchen, they were pleasantly surprised to see all her siblings grinning from ear to ear! Even Mem couldn't hide the joy of seeing them. She offered them leftovers from lunch which they politely declined, saying, "Thanks, but we ate on the way here."

The excitement of showing off their new home soon overtook even her parents. Laura could not wait to show off her new room upstairs.

Rosanna attempted to hide her shocked expression when she walked into Laura's room. She had never seen such a beautiful room in her parents' house. On the wall, there was a lovely drawing of a colorful flower garden neatly framed, showing off Laura's amazing artistic talent. The dresser was adorned with a candle and a beautiful glass dish that Rosanna remembered had been a gift from their grandmother when Laura became a teenager. Her heart was bursting with joy that Laura was allowed to enjoy some ordinary freedoms.

When they returned to the living room, Dat offered them a seat on the couch where the menfolk were visiting. However, there was still more to see, so Mem, Laura, and her excited younger sisters showed Rosanna around the kitchen, the big pantry, and the washhouse. She was thrilled to see their church regulations allowed them to enjoy built-in kitchen cabinets and running water.

Coming back into the living room, they led her to a hallway closet where Mem pulled out a box and handed it to Rosanna. "We never gave you a wedding gift, so this is for you," she smiled.

Rosanna's throat tightened! Never in her wildest dreams did she expect a gift! She was ecstatic beyond words! It was the most precious of all her wedding gifts - a shiny high-quality silverware set for four. She was tempted to kiss the gift since she knew a hug would make Mem uncomfortable, but instead, all she could do was thank her profusely!

They spent the rest of the afternoon visiting, but with a hint of reservation. Dat and Mem both considered it their responsibility to admonish them, although now with kindness.

"We wish you could be happy to live here in our new community. It's different from where you grew up," Dat said, hoping they would be attracted to the relaxed church regulations they had now. But Paul assured him that he and Rosanna enjoyed the life and home in which they were living.

Before they realized it, the evening had slipped away, and it was time to eat a few bites before they needed to get back on the road toward home. The Amish shunning rules restricted the family from eating with Paul and Rosanna at the table. Although Rosanna was never a church member, they shunned her as well. To avoid a rather awkward situation, their best option was to eat cafeteria style. Despite the circumstances, they were thankful to share a meal with the family again.

Rosanna could hardly remember the last time she had eaten her mem's delicious cooking, including her homemade pies. Paul especially enjoyed a big slice of homemade bread as he gave it a lashing of butter, followed by a smothering of homemade strawberry jam. No one would leave the table hungry!

At last, it was time for the goodbyes again. Rosanna strongly disliked that aspect of a visit, and this time was no different. Her siblings' sad smiles tugged at her heartstrings. They would grow up so much before she would see them again.

As they drove onto the gravel road and headed south toward the interstate, Rosanna could contain her pent-up emotions no longer. With tears of gratitude, she showed Paul their wedding gift from her parents. He rejoiced with her, understanding her emotions.

"My heart is overflowing! It's not really the gift itself, but her thoughtfulness. I did not expect this, nor the warm reception for us tonight," she chuckled through tears of happiness.

"God answered our prayers tonight, didn't He? It's a miracle how much their hearts have softened towards us," Paul said.

"Yes, we must never stop praying for them. …*with God, all things are possible,* Matthew 19:26," Rosanna replied, reciting one of their favorite Bible verses. They both wanted to stay on the cloud on which they were floating.

They arrived home shortly after midnight, tired, yet greatly encouraged with the break-through in their family relationship. Rosanna looked forward to sharing their exciting news with the Waltons at church the next day. They would be delighted to hear of the answered prayers and the warm reception received at their family's home in Indiana.

Twenty
CHAPTER 20

Before Paul and Rosanna realized it, Christmas time was upon them again. They had David and Miriam on their mind that holiday season. "Would they allow us to bring a small gift to baby Marvin for Christmas? Maybe we'll get a gift so adorable they won't be able to refuse it," Rosanna chuckled.

The baby department in the mall was unfamiliar territory for Paul and Rosanna. The choices were overwhelming. Spoiling her little nephew looked easy and definitely tempting in the big toy store. Toys, toys, and more toys! It was not a place for the indecisive one. Paul's head was spinning by the time they settled on a small fluffy, gray elephant and a *Baby's First Book*.

Rosanna could already imagine baby Marvin enjoying his little gift! She carefully wrapped the special gift in the perfect box before tucking it neatly among the other gifts under their first beautifully decorated Christmas tree. They would not tell David and Miriam where the gift had been. There was no need to risk offending them with the mention of a "worldly tree."

She felt like a little girl again, counting down the days until Christmas Eve.

The next few days left little time after work for Rosanna to prepare food for the Christmas carry-in dinner at church. Her heart filled with gratitude as she remembered her mem's patience in the kitchen when growing up. Her hands-on training proved rewarding every day as she cooked her husband's favorite meals.

At last it was Christmas Eve! Rosanna was nearly overwhelmed with excitement! As she held the gift on her lap, she thought the short drive to David's house seemed unusually long. She whispered a prayer as they entered the driveway, "Lord, let this visit go well, please."

Paul opened her car door and took her hand. "It will be alright. If they have to reject it, they'll still appreciate the thought," he said, calming her heart.

They stepped onto the front porch, and before they reached the door, David opened it and welcomed them inside. It relieved Rosanna to see Miriam's friendly smile.

Rosanna glanced around. *Where was little Marvin? And her brother Ben?*

Seeing her questioning glance, Miriam hurried to explain, "Marvin is taking a nap right now since he wasn't feeling well. He'll probably be awake soon."

"Oh, sorry to hear that," said Rosanna, trying to hide her eagerness to present the Christmas gift she brought with her."

Offering them a seat in the living room, Miriam continued, "Yes, Marvin caught some sickness circulating among the kids at church. It's rough on the little ones," she said, glancing curiously at the gift in Rosanna's hands. "And Ben went to see one of his friends tonight."

Soon they heard Marvin whimper from the bedroom. Miriam jumped up to tend to him, and returned shortly with her groggy-eyed, chubby little toddler.

He had grown so much since Rosanna had last seen him. He instantly grabbed her heart when he gave her the sweetest smile a sick child could offer from his mem's lap.

She could wait no longer. "Is it alright if we give Marvin a small Christmas gift?" she asked.

She was relieved when Miriam looked at David, and he nodded, "Oh, sure!"

Marvin hesitated to sit on Rosanna's lap, but eventually he assumed it was worth the risk when he saw the shiny package she was holding.

Rosanna sensed the gift was a success when his eyes lit up as he hugged the fluffy elephant to his chest with one hand while trying to look at the little book in the other. Paul and Rosanna were both thrilled with the pleased smiles and a hardy thank you from his parents.

After a while, Rosanna turned to David and asked if he had heard of any recent updates from Indiana.

"Well, it sounds like Dat is not doing well since his heart attack two weeks ago," David informed her. "They put activity restrictions on him, which is not good news."

"No, that does not sound good," Rosanna agreed. Her heart was heavy. She was not only concerned about his physical heart condition, but his spiritual condition as well. *We must go see him again soon. Perhaps he would be open to the Gospel now.*

David's next remark interrupted her thoughts.

"We don't know how much longer Dat will be with us, but I would like to see him have peace about his eternal destiny before it's too late. He says he tried to live righteously to the best of his ability. He hopes God's grace will cover his failures," David said soberly.

Paul and Rosanna both nearly fell off their chairs! *What did David just say? Is he serious? He is disturbed about Dat's soul too?*

When they recovered from the shock of his words, Paul asked, "How do you suggest Dat would find that peace with God?"

"He'd have to trust in Christ for salvation. He paid our sin debt by His death, burial, and resurrection," David proclaimed.

Paul let out a chuckle of delight! "How did you come to this conclusion?"

"Well, that sister of mine was quite the preacher before she left!" David smiled as he winked at Rosanna. She giggled happily. "You were supposed to be joining the church, but instead you were trying to indoctrinate the rest of us with your 'heresy,' as we labeled it. But it convicted me more than I wanted to admit. I wanted to have an Amish wedding, and I feared Miriam would abandon me if she got a hint," he winked at his wife.

Paul and Rosanna eagerly listened for more!

David continued, "Then Clemens stopped by again after our parents moved away. I took that opportunity to ask him about some lingering questions Miriam and I had. All that to say, we've never been the same since that visit, and life is slowly taking on a new meaning for us."

"Do Dat and Mem know about this? How about Ben, since he is working for you and living here?" Rosanna asked.

"Oh, how could I forget to tell you?" David exclaimed. "Yes, Ben is on board with us too. I wish he would be here to speak for himself tonight. He'd love to see you!"

Rosanna was beaming with excitement and wondered if she was dreaming for a moment! *This news is almost too good to be true!*

"And no," David continued, "we're not ready to break the news to our parents yet, especially with Dat's condition right now."

"Well, this certainly is wonderful news! Keep searching the Scriptures, David. The Holy Spirit will reveal the Truth to those who truly want it, no matter the cost," Paul encouraged them as he and Rosanna regretfully prepared to leave.

They were barely on the road when Paul and Rosanna cheered and rejoiced again over the new names written in Heaven! "God has answered another prayer!" Paul cheered. "Yes, what a great encouragement!" Rosanna added as she looked forward to making more visits to David and Miriam's house soon.

They took an alternate route home and stopped by to wish Paul's parents a Merry Christmas as well. Their visits with them were usually cordial and uneventful. His parents were grieved with Paul's abandoning of the Amish faith, but remained thankful he still believed in God.

Several months later in early spring time, Paul and Rosanna were disheartened to learn that Dat's health had declined even further. They felt burdened to go see him again soon. She specifically asked God to give her some time alone with her dat to share the Gospel with him again.

Their visit with her family was pleasantly peaceful. In the afternoon, when everyone else was occupied outside, Rosanna seized the opportunity to spend an hour at her dat's bedside by herself.

Again, she explained to him the lost condition of all mankind and the remedy - Christ's redeeming sacrifice at Calvary. "We cannot add to His finished work on the cross by being Amish or anything else. In John 19:30, Jesus said, '*It is finished…*' Dat, He wants us to receive His forgiveness and trust in Him alone for eternal life and a home in Heaven," she reminded him.

Dat listened intently, but with little response. She realized only God could give him the understanding of his need for salvation. However, Rosanna felt privileged to have shared the Truth with him once more. God had graciously granted her wish to spend personal time with him.

Mem, strong and energetic, made certain her husband was well cared for daily. "I have a good hope that he is prepared for Heaven," she assured Rosanna. "He has been a faithful Amish church member and lived righteously to the best of his knowledge and ability."

Rosanna was reminded again of how securely Mem was anchored in the man-made belief system. Obviously, only the Holy Spirit could convince her of the Gospel

Truth. Yet, she could not imagine anyone, even God, breaking through Mem's concrete wall of defense for the Amish-designed hope of Heaven.

However, Rosanna would never give up. *As long as there was life and a sound mind, there was a possibility for one to turn to Christ. But would it ever happen?* She would continue to pray for her parents and siblings, and wait on the God of all miracles to do what only He could do.

Twenty-one
CHAPTER 21

The hot summer sun was bearing down as David stacked bundles of wheat on the wooden farm wagon to haul to the thrashing machine beside the barn. Heavy drops of sweat dripped off the horses, and they didn't want to move until they were commanded to do so. He could not help but wonder if it might be his last summer to endure this kind of fieldwork.

David and Miriam's new beliefs had eventually leaked out to the public, and the inevitable was almost upon them. It would only be a matter of time until their circumstances would demand a major change. *How long will we be tolerated in the church? What will our future hold?* they wondered.

A month later, just when Dat and Mem thought their family's disgrace had been diminished in the new community, they received a letter from David and Miriam about their church situation. Although his parents were aware of their doubts of the Amish religion, they had hoped to never receive such a letter. *How could it be!*

Making matters worse, Mem's fears of David and Miriam's influence on Ben were not unfounded. He was in agreement with their objections to the Amish teachings. Mem immediately knew the consequences. Two more of their children would be shunned and the family would be further torn apart. They would not be able to enjoy their first grandchild as much anymore.

With the letter in hand, she collapsed into the nearby rocking chair, weeping uncontrollably. Dat had not yet read it, but tried to comfort her. "What happened? Maybe it will be alright."

"No, Dat, it won't be alright," she said, as she wept until she had exhausted her energy for the rest of the afternoon.

After reading the letter, Dat agreed that she was right. *What horrible, heart-breaking news!*

Mem could never have imagined the pain of one's heart being shattered into a thousand pieces, not only once or twice, but thrice. She felt her heart was completely and irreparably fragmented.

That afternoon and evening, Laura and her siblings took over the housework and let Mem rest and grieve with Dat. Everyone at the dinner table seemed to pick and nibble at their food, rather than devour it as usual. Mem understood. Sad hearts curb the appetite.

David and Miriam were dreading their future visits with the family, knowing that different biblical views would be sure to clash. *If the Amish religion is based on God's Word as they profess, why must it be so divisive?* they lamented.

* * * *

Soon the leaves of the trees were softly waving their beautiful autumn colors again. It was Rosanna's favorite time of the year and it was about to become even more special to her. She had left her job at the day care and was eager to meet their own newborn baby soon. They wondered how many days of waiting remained until they would become brand new parents.

Paul and Rosanna always looked forward to driving out to the country since they could now enjoy the fellowship with her two siblings who still lived in the area. They were on one of those visits when Rosanna suddenly realized that she was having some unusual pains. She looked at Paul and whispered urgently, "I think we'd better leave!"

Noting the alarm on her face, he jumped up from his chair and announced it was time to go home. In keeping with the Amish customs, they didn't mention her labor pains to the guys, but Rosanna took Miriam aside and said, "It looks like we might be going to the hospital tonight. I'm having frequent contractions."

"Oh, I'm so happy for you! Let us know when the baby comes!" Miriam was giddy with excitement.

Paul drove extra carefully all the way home. He was more nervous than Rosanna. "Do you think that we should go straight to the hospital?" he asked, alarm in his voice.

"I think we'll wait to see how it progresses at home. We're only minutes away from the hospital," she smiled.

Paul kept a watchful eye on her for the next few hours. Shortly before midnight when she was doubled over in misery, and he had reached panic mode, Paul said, "We're going to the hospital before this little one makes her appearance here at home."

While Rosanna packed a few last things in her bag, Paul nervously paced the floor. When she was ready, he carefully helped her into the car and threw the bag in the back seat beside the baby carrier. Then he swiftly ran around the car, jumped in, and threw it into drive.

As they sped down the street, he frequently glanced at Rosanna. Her expressions were keeping him updated.

They arrived at the hospital exactly seven minutes later. After another strong contraction, she smiled at Paul and reminded him that keeping calm would be a great help. "Remember, it's me having the baby!" They both paused for a good laugh.

After the next contraction, he took her hand and walked her through the front doors of the hospital. They were grateful that she was admitted shortly.

While the nurses cared for her, Paul finally sat down and let reality sink in. They would soon meet their precious little one! The clock seemed to move ever so slowly.

Adding to each agonizing contraction was the pain of her mem's absence at such a significant moment in her life. However, she willingly faced the sacrifice she was called to make as a result of choosing to serve her risen Savior.

Several long hours later the delivery was imminent. Seeing his lovely wife in misery was hard to bear. Paul felt helpless! All he could do was stay by her side, pray, hold her hand, and kiss her forehead.

At 4:20 in the morning, cheers erupted in the delivery room as the squirming, dark-haired baby Hannah Grace entered the world.

Paul and Rosanna had never seen a baby more beautiful! They were amazed at her chubby little face, and could hardly get enough snuggles with their cuddly bundle of joy. God, the Creator, had designed her so perfectly.

Mid-morning, the Waltons came beaming into the room carrying a giant gift bag full of useful and cute baby gifts. Their visit reminded Paul and Rosanna of how much they appreciated their friendship and of the void they filled as their "foster" parents. Rosanna watched tearfully as Mrs. Walton wasted no time in cuddling the little bundle in her arms. How she longed to show off little Hannah to her own parents and siblings!

The Waltons had barely exited the room when David and Miriam appeared with radiant smiles. It warmed Rosanna's heart to have at least one family member come to rejoice with them.

Rosanna and baby Hannah were doing well, and after a few days, Paul received permission to take them home.

Life had definitely changed for them. They faced new adjustments every day for the next several weeks and months.

When Hannah was a month old, they decided to visit Rosanna's family in Indiana. *Surely, they'd be eager to see their new granddaughter and niece.* David and Miriam agreed to join them on the journey, while Ben stayed home to care for the farm and animals. They prayed again for a peaceful visit.

Rosanna and her brother were saddened when they arrived at their parents' house and learned that their dat's condition had worsened again. He was not the spry Dat and strong farmer they used to know.

Rosanna also detected an underlying sadness in her mem, although outwardly she appeared to enjoy seeing them. Though plain color, their non-Amish clothes seemed to add to her grieved spirit. *The consequence of a man-made religion.*

Rosanna's attention was quickly shifted to the rest of her family as they crowded around her to get their first glimpse of baby Hannah. She wanted her mem to hold Hannah first. "Grandmothers should always be at the front of the waiting line to hold her new grandbaby!" Rosanna teased her siblings.

In the meantime, Marvin got his share of attention from his aunts and uncles. He was no longer the little guy they had known before they moved to Indiana. Now, he was an energetic toddler running throughout the house.

Aside from the obligatory shunning at mealtimes, the rest of the visit was more pleasant than expected. They spent the next day together entertaining the grandbabies and touring the farm.

It was late in the afternoon as they prepared to leave when Mem disappeared into her bedroom and soon returned with a gift for both grandbabies. She smiled, handing a toy to Marvin and a pink baby blanket to Rosanna for baby Hannah. Miriam and Rosanna joyfully thanked her, and Marvin was thrilled to have his own toy to take home!

When they were finally moving towards the door in efforts to leave, Mem could not resist the typical reminder. "We wish things were still like it used to be. Aren't you ready to come back yet? We didn't train you to live out in the world. Remember your promise you made in baptism to uphold the church rules," she reminded them sadly.

Secretly, Rosanna was thankful again that no one could use baptism and church membership to lay guilt on her. She glanced at Paul and David, waiting for either of them to respond.

Should they try to explain the Gospel of salvation once more? David wondered, understanding Rosanna's glance. He cleared his throat and began, "Mem, we believe what the Bible says about trusting Jesus alone for eternal life. In Acts 4:12 it says, *Neither is there salvation in any other; for there is none other name under heaven given among men, whereby we must be saved.* By faith we believe that is true. '*No other name*' means not even Amish."

Paul, Rosanna, and Miriam nodded in agreement as they listened to David speak.

Mem had been listening intently and was clearly disturbed by David's words. She moved closer to him as if to make her point more persuasive. "Yes, we must have faith," Mem replied, "but again I must say that faith involves many things. If we do not obey God's commandments, follow the church guidelines as we promised, and separate from the world, to name a few, then it's evident that we are not following Christ."

David tried to clarify once again, "Mem, it seems you are misunderstanding us. It is our sincere desire to obey God's Word and follow His leading - not to earn salvation, but as a result of having received salvation. Salvation is not a reward or something earned. The true evidence of a born again believer is the fruit of the Spirit, which He produces through us by His spirit and not by the '*works of the flesh*' according to Galatians 5:20."

"David, it sounds like you have let yourself become confused with the scriptures by not staying faithful to your upbringing," Mem responded as she shook her head and remained unconvinced yet again.

Rosanna looked at Paul hopelessly, knowing the discussion was going nowhere fast! She got the impression they could talk in circles well into the night and accomplish nothing. *But would God's Word return void? Could the Spirit be working where we can not see?* She could not help but wonder. *Perhaps He would work in the hearts of my siblings who listened intently.* She was surprised that Mem allowed them to be present for this discussion.

From where he was sitting in his chair on the other side of the room, Dat had also been listening and agreeing with Mem. Seeing that it was getting late for their drive home, he interrupted suddenly, "Well, we'd better let you go. Let's leave some visiting for next time."

They all chuckled, glad to hear he still had his wonderful sense of humor!

"Yes, I believe you're right, Dat. We need to be going," Paul said as he reached for Hannah's diaper bag on the chair. "It's getting late for a long drive."

After repeated goodbyes and hugs for the babies, they were homeward bound. Rosanna had a sense of satisfaction from their visit -- having done what they could to share the gospel, and trusting the Lord with the results.

David and Miriam were expelled from the Amish church soon after coming home from their trip with Paul and Rosanna to Indiana. Riding with a shunned former church member was a major offense and called for church discipline.

Ben was aware that his turn to be excommunicated was coming next if he did not recant. Having understood his need, he had also repented and received the Savior. He already knew what his choice would be, and it was made easier by the fact that he did not yet have a girlfriend.

* * * *

As the next few months gradually turned into winter, the holidays were upon them once again. Rosanna looked forward to spending Christmas dinner with David and Miriam for the first time since they left the Amish culture.

A few days before Christmas, Clemens came to visit David and Miriam again. He was thrilled to hear that Ben was also on his way out of the Amish religion. He also found his way to Paul and Rosanna's house in town and rejoiced with them for answered prayers concerning David, Miriam, and Ben.

"Rosanna," Clemens addressed her, "on my first visit to your parent's house years ago, I thought I was in a dead end conversation talking to your mem. She seemed to reject every word of Scripture that I shared with her. I assumed my time spent there was in vain.

"But here you are today, Rosanna, along with two of your siblings, free from the bondage of sin - the blessed result of God drawing you to Himself on that day! What an awesome God we serve!" Clemens was ecstatic!

"Yes," Rosanna replied heartily, "thank you for caring enough for our souls to come share the Gospel Truths with us!" She could not adequately express her gratitude for his faithfulness to the Lord.

"What a blessed little girl Hannah is to be born to parents who blazed the trail for her. May she come to realize her need for the Savior at a young age. I know you will train her well," Clemens said encouragingly.

"By God's grace, we pray Hannah and any future children will always love and serve the Lord. We are eager to see what God's plan will be for her," Rosanna smiled.

Twenty-two

CHAPTER 22

"Hello, this is Rosanna."

When she answered the phone on a snowy January morning, she did not expect it to turn her day upside down.

"Hi, Rosanna, this is your parents' neighbor, Chuck. Your mom asked me to let you know that your dad is in the hospital - he's had a heart attack. The doctors said the prognosis is not good. I'm sorry I don't have better news for you."

Speechless, she sat in a nearby chair.

"Rosanna, are you there?" Chuck asked after a few seconds of silence from Rosanna.

"Y-Yes, thanks for letting me know," she stammered. "Do you have any more details?"

"No, sorry I don't have more details," he said.

"Tell my mother to keep us updated, please."

She stayed in the chair for several minutes, too stunned to move. *How can it be?*

She dropped to her knees on the kitchen floor. In tears she pleaded, "Lord, don't let him die yet, please. Give him an understanding of his need to be reconciled with you before it's too late, if he hasn't settled that yet. Refresh his mind of the Truths we've shared with him."

When she had composed herself, she remembered to call Paul and her brothers with the sad news. They all prayed fervently that he would accept Christ before it was forever too late. What a comfort it was to Paul and Rosanna to know that even their church family was in prayer for her dat!

The daily updates from Chuck indicated no improvement in her father's health. Burdened for him, Paul agreed to take Rosanna and Ben to visit him at the hospital. David and Miriam left the following day, after they had arranged for the neighbors to take over the farm chores and keep the fire going in their wood stove.

Arriving at the hospital, they found that Mem had gone home for a few hours to check on things and had asked Laura to stay with Dat until she returned.

Dat seemed unresponsive as Rosanna spoke to him. "Dat, can you hear me? This is Rosanna. I love you, and I have been praying for you."

He opened his eyes ever so slightly and then drifted off again. Rosanna tried a second time, while Paul and Ben watched from the other side of the bed. "Dat, are you awake?" she asked. He nodded slightly.

"Dat, I need to ask you a question. Do you remember what we had shared about everyone's need for a Savior? Have you asked Jesus to forgive your sins and be your Savior? If you ask Him to, He will forgive you, save you, and give you a home in Heaven.

"Remember John 3:16? *For God So loved the world that he gave his only begotten son, that whosoever believeth in him should not perish but have everlasting life,*" she quoted to him.

He stirred with a faint, but brief smile on his face. Rosanna wanted to believe it was a positive response to her question, but she realized only God knew his heart.

Her siblings agreed - there was nothing more they could do.

Within the hour, Mem returned to find them all around Dat's bed. She was delighted that Paul, Rosanna, and Ben could come so soon.

As his condition declined that evening, they called David and Miriam to encourage them to come as soon as possible. They prayed he would survive until they arrived.

After a full clinical assessment the next morning, his doctor estimated that he might have merely hours to live. The children who were still at home were brought to the hospital after completing their chores and breakfast. David and Miriam arrived early in the afternoon.

As they all gathered around his bedside, they sang his favorite hymn of "Amazing Grace." They continued with "I'll Fly Away" and "What a Friend We Have in Jesus." It was a bittersweet time for the family as songs and tears mingled with goodbyes.

Shortly after eight o'clock that evening they witnessed him drawing his last breath. His life on this side of eternity had ceased forever.

Rosanna struggled to grasp the dreadful finality of losing her dat. She had never imagined that parting with a close family member could cause so much pain. Paul remained close by her side to comfort her throughout the day.

Knowing that God was her ultimate strength, a scripture passage came to mind--2 Corinthians 12:9 where Paul wrote of Christ, *My grace is sufficient for thee: for my strength is made perfect in weakness...*

The next few days were filled with hundreds of relatives and friends coming and going. Rosanna had nearly forgotten how the traditional Amish visitation and funeral consisted of great crowds of people coming to give their condolences and love to the bereaved.

On the day of the funeral service, the non-Amish siblings were not expecting the special blessing God had in store for them.

Although they were family, they had expected the usual Amish shunning policy in which they grew up to dictate the day. Traditionally, shunned family members would be seated in the farthest corner of the house in which the funeral was being held. Most often, they would be in a separate room from the rest of the family.

To their great surprise, in this new community, Mem felt the liberty to allow them to sit with the rest of the family next to the casket. All her children were seated in their birth order. She received criticism from some of the ultra-conservative Amish relatives for being too lenient and kind toward her non-Amish children. They feared the strict shunning, designed to deter others from following the wayward ones, could lose its effectiveness.

However, Rosanna sensed a renewed family closeness, and her heart was overflowing with joy and sorrow simultaneously. The very real presence of the Lord sustained her throughout the difficult day of burying her dat.

That afternoon, as they sat and observed the camaraderie of more than fifty Amish and non-Amish cousins, Paul commented, "Rosanna, look at this! Only God could have worked such a miracle!"

The time for Rosanna and her siblings' trek back home came much too quickly the following day. Parting was more difficult than ever. They wondered how Mem and their siblings would navigate the difficult and lonely days ahead.

Rosanna promised the rest of the family that she would be much in prayer for them. Mem assured her that she would be fine over time, although it would be hard.

* * * *

The weeks turned into months, and the routine of life continued as they approached spring and summer once more.

Paul and Rosanna missed being able to go out to the old homestead during the summer harvest time as they were accustomed to doing before her family had moved away. However, they still enjoyed an occasional drive through the countryside on a calm summer evening. It was relaxing and brought back many memories. They would often stop at David and Miriam's house or visit one of the Amish neighbors.

On one such drive, they stopped at Eli's farm. He was a friend of Paul's from his teenage years. The afternoon was sultry and Eli was just finishing up a day of baling hay with a horse-drawn baler. Paul felt sorry for him now, knowing there were more convenient and faster methods to bale hay - and all with a guilt-free conscience.

Eli did not seem to appreciate being reminded of that fact. He assumed that he had no other options and was willing to abide by the rules, even if it meant doing things the old-fashioned way.

"Yeah, here we are working hard and sweating out in the blazing sun, and we don't even have 'salvation.' All the while, you people can sit in an air conditioned tractor cab and supposedly be on your way to Heaven," Eli remarked with a sneer.

Paul felt the sting of sarcasm in his voice and realized that Eli was not even aware of the truth of his own statement. *You are exactly right, if you're depending on your lifestyle to prepare you for Heaven,* he thought.

However, refraining from telling him as much, he simply remarked, "The choice is yours."

"Choice?" Eli questioned in shock, glaring at Paul.

"Yes, and I'll pray you will get to experience the choice of freedom someday, Buddy," Paul responded with a grin as he turned to leave.

Twenty-three
CHAPTER 23

Summer ended with great excitement for Paul and Rosanna. It was the day they had anticipated for nine months.

"It's a boy!" The nurses cheered as the couple greeted their first son with sheer delight. Even the doctor was awed by little Micah's full head of dark hair. "It's not surprising since both sides of the family have mostly dark hair," Rosanna chuckled.

Little Hannah could hardly get enough of him, as she tried to help welcome her little brother with childish hugs and slobbery kisses.

The hospital stay was short, and they were glad to be home to enjoy their new family. More adjustments and challenges surfaced for Rosanna as she learned to juggle her housework, cooking, and caring for her two little ones. Paul helped as much as possible every day after he came home from work.

When Micah was ten weeks old, Paul and Rosanna's faith was tested like never before. They noticed a sudden change in Micah's health. He became fussy and began to show all the symptoms of a severe cold. Having observed her mem successfully treat many illnesses at home, Rosanna used what she had been taught to help her baby feel better. However, when he developed a high fever and refused to eat, they realized he needed medical attention.

The doctor's diagnosis was not good news. Micah's little fevered body was trying to fight a respiratory infection and pneumonia. He was admitted to the small local hospital for treatment. However, when he failed to respond quickly to the medication, he was transported by ambulance to a larger hospital seventy-five miles away.

Paul and Rosanna were tempted to question why God would let this happen to their precious little son. All they could do was pray to the Great Physician for his recovery. "Thy will be done" was never harder to utter in their prayers. They were heartbroken as they helplessly watched him suffer. The support of love and prayers from the Waltons and their church family helped carry them through each unpromising day.

Placing Hannah in the care of church friends was comforting, yet being many miles away was painfully difficult. How they longed to be there for both of their babies! Paul would make the long trip back to see her periodically. But she also sorely missed her mommy, which tore at Rosanna's already hurting heart.

Slowly but surely, over the first five days, Micah's condition began improving in response to the medications and many prayers. Only then was Hannah allowed to come with her daddy to the hospital for a visit. There her mommy wrapped her in her arms, never wanting to let go again!

After ten long days of uncertainty, Micah's condition improved enough that the doctors felt it was safe to let him go home and their family was reunited once again. It seemed like the happiest day of their life!

In a few weeks, Micah was a happy little boy again. Paul and Rosanna promised themselves they would never take healthy children for granted again.

* * * *

Paul's job called for a business trip to Michigan a month later. He knew it would be the perfect time to take

Rosanna and the children along to spend time with her mem in Indiana.

Rosanna was excited for the opportunity. She could spend an entire day with her mem and siblings for the first time since her dat's funeral. She prayed that it would be a special time with Mem, a time to renew their relationship.

Upon arriving the next week, Rosanna was thankful to see that Mem and the children had adjusted well to their new normal without Dat. She painfully missed him greeting them when they arrived. Mem and the siblings were thrilled to meet little Micah, and they welcomed him with open arms.

Rosanna could not keep from reflecting on her first visit to their house after she had left the Amish community. Their friendly reception was a welcome contrast to the rejection she had received in the early days of her new life. It encouraged her to see how God had worked in their hearts! She was sure she could trust Him to do so much more in the coming years to bring their family back together again.

Rosanna prayed for an open door to be a witness to her mem. *One never knows when it could be the last time,* she reminded herself. She was given that opportunity when her younger siblings took Hannah outside to play on the swing and to see the farm animals.

Mem quickly seized the opportunity to challenge Rosanna on several Scriptures with a determination to disprove Rosanna's viewpoint. When Rosanna explained once more that salvation is in Christ alone, Mem referred to it as a ticket to sin and a false hope of Heaven.

Mem was also adamant about obeying the "commandments," which she insisted would include the Amish beliefs and lifestyle.

"But Mem, John 3:36 says, *He that believeth on the Son hath everlasting life; and he that believeth not the Son shall not see life; for the wrath of God abideth on him.*"

"Jesus tells us He is the door to Heaven. In John chapter 10, and many other Scriptures, it is clear that He is the only way. We can add nothing of our own goodness to it." It seemed to Rosanna that she had reminded her mem of this numerous times already, yet she still refused to hear it.

Mem insisted that Rosanna was still misunderstanding the Bible. "One must be in the right standing to receive God's grace, which includes obedience," she stated firmly.

"The Bible says in Ephesians 2:8 that we are saved *by grace through faith.* We can't earn grace, or else it becomes works. Grace is an undeserved favor from God to mankind."

Rosanna paused and walked to the door to check on Hannah. Micah was still napping peacefully. As she started toward the kitchen, Mem asked her to wait while she got a paper and pencil.

"Now, Rosanna, I'm not finished with our discussion. I'm not saying I agree with you, but I want you to write down all the Scriptures you quoted to me so I can look them up."

"Well, it probably won't be much help if you've already rejected it," Rosanna reminded her respectfully.

"No, I just want to see why and how you could perceive these Scriptures the way you do," Mem said, a bit flustered.

"Oh, okay." Rosanna had a ray of hope that the Holy Spirit had not given up on her mem. Perhaps He was still working in her heart.

Rosanna found a piece of paper in her Bible to jot down the Scripture references. But Mem refused the paper and retrieved her own note paper from the desk. Her version of shunning would not allow taking even a piece of Rosanna's own paper. *She must have forgotten momentarily that I was never a church member, thus eliminating the need to shun.*

Paul returned the next day to pick up Rosanna and the children. After the usual goodbyes, they were securely buckled in for the trip back home. As they sped down the highway, the children soon succumbed to nap time.

Finally, Rosanna could update Paul on her interesting day and her conversation with her mem.

"We need to keep praying for her even more fervently," Paul encouraged her. "Who knows what could grow from the seeds you've planted so many times already. I'm so proud of you for your obedience to God and blazing the trail for others to follow Him. I believe God is not finished yet!"

"You know our favorite quote — 'Nothing is too hard for God!' We know, called upon, He can transform a determined self-righteous heart into a tender regenerate heart. But will she ever understand her need to call upon Him?" *Time would tell.*

Rosanna refused to give up hope for her mem's change of heart.

Twenty-four

CHAPTER 24

One warm summer morning the following year, when Rosanna checked their mailbox, she was ecstatic. *A letter from Mem! I can't believe it!* She had given up hope of getting a response to the birthday card and letter she had sent her in the spring.

She eagerly ripped it open to find a three-page handwritten letter inside. Hoping it was all good news, she nestled herself comfortably on the couch to enjoy her first letter ever from her mem.

Oh, wonderful! Laura and Raymond are getting married in October, she smiled. "We would love to have you here for the wedding, but as you know, the church does not allow us to invite you. I'm sorry it has to be this way," she read.

Rosanna felt the painful sting of shunning when she imagined the first of her sisters getting married without her. Yet she was not surprised that they were not invited. *But at least she desired to have us there, which is unusual for her to admit. Is Mem perhaps still processing grief and experiencing loneliness since Dat passed away?* she wondered. As she finished reading the letter, she had a renewed burden and concern for her mem.

With the letter in her lap, Rosanna sat staring out the window; her thoughts far away in Indiana. She resolved to respond to the letter soon and try to encourage her if possible.

Rosanna did not expect to hear from Mem again until after Laura's wedding when the busyness slowed down.

The time seemed to drag on as she waited. After a couple months and still no letter, she began to wonder, *will I ever receive a letter from Mem again?*

Two weeks after the wedding, she was alarmed when the phone rang late one afternoon from an Indiana phone number. *A call from home?* Her heart started racing! *Oh! perhaps Mem had decided to call rather than writing.* She eagerly picked up the phone.

"Hello, this is Rosanna," she said politely.

"Hi, it's Laura," she heard on the other end of the line as her own smile faded. She was startled to hear Laura's nervous voice instead of her mem. *What was going on?*

"Yes, Laura. How are you? Is everything okay?" Rosanna asked all in one breath.

"No! I'm calling from the hospital." Laura's voice was filled with emotion. A thousand thoughts rushed through Rosanna's mind in the next few seconds as she waited for what seemed like five minutes before Laura was able to continue.

"Mem was in a bad accident on the way home from town this afternoon when a speeding pickup truck popped over the big hill on Highway 16. The driver failed to see her rig in time to avoid running into the back of her buggy. She was thrown out onto the road and was hurt very badly. We don't know the full extent of her injuries yet, but she has head injuries and broken bones in addition to internal injuries." Laura paused to catch her breath. "She is in surgery here at Mercy hospital right now," she added with a sniffle.

Rosanna was speechless! At last she responded with a heavy heart, "I'm so sorry to hear that! Is she going to be alright?" she asked tearfully. "Were you able to see her before the surgery?"

"Yes, I saw her briefly before they took her into the operating room, but she was not coherent. Pray her head injuries are not too severe," Laura said, still in shock.

"She will certainly be in our prayers, and I'm sure we will try to go see her at the hospital as soon as possible," Rosanna assured her.

"Please, come as soon as you can," Laura pleaded. With all differences aside, she needed the support from her sister more than ever at such a heartbreaking time.

"Keep us updated, and we will see you soon," Rosanna said tenderly.

"We will update you in the morning," Laura promised. "I will call David and Ben and let them know as well," she added.

After Rosanna laid down her cell phone, she looked at Hannah and Micah playing at her feet. *The innocence of a child, oblivious to the cares and worries of the world around them!*

I must remember to take all my cares, including Mem, to the Lord and leave them there, she reminded herself even as her tears spilled over and her own emotions nearly overtook her.

When Paul came home an hour later, she quickly informed him of the bad news and the details about Mem. He was stunned as well and tried to comfort Rosanna as they immediately prayed together for God's grace concerning Mem. They thanked Him for His mercy in sparing Mem's life and giving her another opportunity to call upon Him before it was eternally too late.

"We need to go see her as soon as possible," Paul said, understanding Rosanna's eagerness to be with her family. "However, maybe we should wait until tomorrow morning when we get an update," he suggested, and Rosanna agreed.

Early the following morning, Laura called again as promised. Rosanna had hoped for a report of improvement.

"Mem is about the same," she said. "The good news is that the doctor said her head injuries are not as severe as we had feared at first. The bad news is she is still in critical care since the surgery and obviously in much pain even while on pain medication. If she makes significant improvements today she might be able to move to a regular room soon. Please, pray that no complications develop."

After Laura's call, Paul and Rosanna hurriedly finished breakfast and attended to last minute details before leaving. As soon as they had the luggage loaded into the car and the little ones buckled into their seats, they were on their way to Indiana.

Rosanna once again glanced at her sleeping babies in the back seat. *The sweet innocence of a child allows them a peaceful sleep despite the troubled world around them.* She laid her head back for the tenth time trying to take a nap only to be occupied by hundreds of thoughts chasing through her mind like a race track.

Opening her eyes again, she noticed the glaring numbers of the digital clock in the car dash were seemingly stuck on eleven o'clock. *Shouldn't it be at least noon by now?*

When they arrived at the hospital waiting room that afternoon, the newlyweds, Raymond and Laura, were waiting for them. Laura was glad to inform them that Mem had made some improvements, and she was able to communicate briefly with her. However, she was allowed only one visitor at a time while in critical care.

Rosanna asked Paul to take his turn first to go in. She had a feeling her visit might take a good while. She prayed for wisdom as she waited to see Mem.

Twenty-five

CHAPTER 25

Rosanna's heart broke as she stood at Mem's bedside, her eyes overflowing at the sight of the daunting network of tubes and wires attached to Mem's battered and bruised body. *Her condition must be worse than I heard!* As she wiped the tears from her cheeks, she reached down and softly touched Mem's arm. Mem slowly opened her eyes and smiled faintly when she saw it was Rosanna instead of the nurse.

"Hi, Mem, how are you feeling?" she asked.

"Not so well."

"Are you in pain?" Rosanna asked.

"Yes. Pray for me," she said, barely above a whisper.

"Yes, I've been praying a lot for you, and so have many other people. We all love you and want you to get well," Rosanna said softly. Mem nodded as well as she could with restricted movement.

Rosanna gently held her hand as she prayed for her in a soft voice. Although Mem was not familiar with praying without the traditional prayer book, she squeezed Rosanna's hand and thanked her.

In a few minutes her limited time to visit ended, but Rosanna promised Mem she would be back soon. *No doubt, for many more days to come,* she thought.

At last, on the morning of the third day, Rosanna was delighted when she walked into the critical care room once more and was just in time to hear Doctor Hayden tell

Mem, "You will be moved to a regular room today! Although you still have a little way to full recovery, I am pleased with the improvements you've made so far," he added.

"That's the best news we've heard since you came here, isn't it, Mem?" Rosanna said through misty eyes as they rejoiced together. She immediately hurried over to the waiting room to tell Paul!

Then she called her mem's closest neighbor, asking her to pass the good news on to Raymond and Laura who lived several miles away from them. *They need to have their own phone!* Rosanna thought as her appreciation for freedom and technology was renewed yet again!

Around mid-morning, David and Miriam's family, along with Ben, arrived at the hospital only for the day. They had responsibilities at home which hindered them from staying as long as they desired. Mem was happy to see them, and they were pleased that she was improving daily and in good spirits. In her typical *mem attitude*, her goal was to recover as fast as possible!

After the school children came home in the afternoon, their neighbor picked them up in her van to go see Mem. Raymond and Laura, who had been babysitting Hannah and Micah, also came long with the children. When the family arrived at the hospital, Mem was settled in her room and sound asleep, but her nap was cut short when the nurse came in to check on her again. Rosanna took the opportunity to tell Mem she had visitors who were eager to see her!

She welcomed her school children in as they cautiously eased up to her bedside, wide-eyed and intimidated by the strange surroundings. Although speechless, their broad smiles spoke of their joy in seeing her.

An hour and a half later, they had all gone home, leaving only Paul and Rosanna's family. Raymond and Laura would return later in the evening to stay for the night. Rosanna was thankful Mem allowed them to stay with her during the day.

When they had finished eating a light meal in the cafeteria, Paul took Hannah and Micah on an entertaining stroller ride while Rosanna went back to check on Mem. Rosanna presumed she would be asleep after her long and tiring day. But when she tip-toed into her room she noticed Mem had her gaze fixed on the view outside the window. Sensing Rosanna's presence, she turned her eyes toward the door.

"Are you enjoying the scenery out there?" Rosanna asked. "I wish you could have a better view than the tall buildings across the street."

"Oh, it's alright. I was just thinking...," Mem left her sentence hanging in mid-air as she absent-mindedly gazed out the window again.

"May I ask what is on your mind?" Rosanna asked casually.

At last, she turned back to Rosanna and continued, " I-I was just thinking… thinking about my accident. It all happened so suddenly! It seems one minute I was riding along, and the next minute emergency personnel were lifting me into the ambulance. I could easily have died. Where would I be right now if God had not worked a miracle and let me live? I don't understand His ways, but I'm so thankful He spared my life."

"Yes, I'm so thankful God let you survive the accident! But are you afraid to die?" Rosanna asked, sympathetically.

She nodded slowly, "I've had doubts, but our Bishop visited me last night after you left, so I asked him how I can have peace about my hope of Heaven.

Rosanna's mouth dropped open. "So what did the Bishop tell you?" she asked.

"He seemed to be positive that if I remain loyal to the church guidelines and to God's Word to the best of my ability, then I can have faith that I will receive eternal life when I die. But I'm not perfect and what if I still fall short?" She looked tiredly into Rosanna's eyes in a desperate plea for affirmation.

Rosanna cringed. It sounded all too familiar. *What a misleading and depressing answer to an all important question*, she thought sadly.

Rosanna pulled her chair up closer to the bedside and held Mem's hand in her own while holding the Bible in her other hand.

"Mem, the Bible tells us that we all fall short of God's standard of perfection according to Romans 3:23, *For all have sinned and come short of the glory of God.*

But we need not be fearful of eternity if we have prepared in God's way, the only way. We should not dare assume that we are going to enter Heaven because we've lived a good life or lived a better life than those around us. The Bible tells us all our own good deeds are as filthy rags in light of salvation. We are sinners as was the tax collector in Luke 18:13, who said, *God, be merciful to me, a sinner!* He had nothing to contribute to his own salvation. All he had was his plea for mercy.

"That is why *God gave His only begotten Son that whosoever believeth in Him should not perish, but have everlasting life,* as John 3:16 says."

"But surely our efforts to please God, helping the poor, and doing good should count for something, wouldn't you say?" Mem asked with a hint of doubt.

"Titus 3:5 says, *Not by works of righteousness which we have done, but according to His mercy He saved us, by the washing of regeneration, and renewing of the Holy Ghost,"* Rosanna read to her.

She paused. Mem was listening, but she did not want to wear her out. Then she nodded for Rosanna to continue.

"So, if we repent of our own ways and put our complete trust in Christ's sacrifice on the cross for forgiveness of our sins, we are reconciled to Him. That is how we become a child of God," Rosanna continued. "Do you remember what Romans 10:13 says?"

Mem furrowed her brow, "No, not really, you'll have to remind me."

"It says, *For whosoever shall call upon the name of the Lord shall be saved,"* Rosanna quoted. "He doesn't leave us hopeless!

"He wants us to have the assurance of salvation after we receive it and not live in doubt. That's why he gave us 1 John 5:13 which says, *These things have I written unto you that believe on the name of the son of God that ye may know that you have eternal life…"*

"Yes, I've heard some of these Scriptures before. But I don't understand what you mean by receiving salvation. How does one receive it?" Mem asked with a puzzled expression.

"That is the same question I asked myself a few years ago," Rosanna smiled. "Then I learned that I will receive salvation when I repent of my own sinful way and ask God to forgive my sins and be my Savior. He has promised it to us if we sincerely ask Him!"

Mem did not respond, but she closed her eyes. Rosanna assumed she must be exhausted and in need of rest.

Immediately, the night shift nurse came in to check on Mem and kindly told Rosanna that it was time to let her rest, and she could come back in the morning.

Rosanna quietly left the room to join Paul in the waiting room. By now, Raymond and Laura had returned and were waiting with him. She was relieved to see that Hannah and Micah were already sound asleep in the stroller.

"Is Mem alright? That seemed like a rather long check up on her," Paul chuckled as Rosanna sat next to him on a lobby chair.

She was barely seated when she dropped her face into her hands and started weeping, releasing her suppressed and mixed emotions!

"What happened? Is Mem getting worse?" They all questioned, alarmed and confused.

"No, it's just that my heart is nearly exploding with joy," she explained as she dried her face.

"Mem was really touched by the fact that God spared her life in the accident. It caused her to be disturbed about her eternal destiny. Depending on her Amish faith was not giving her the peace she had expected to have in such a situation. She had questions and allowed me to talk through several Scriptures with her. I explained what the Bible teaches about man's sinful nature and need of salvation. She listened intently and wondered how to receive the Savior. Then, the nurse came in, and I needed to leave."

Paul rejoiced with her, but Raymond and Laura sat in awkward silence as they tried to decipher Rosanna's strange incident.

Finally, after a few questions and some Scripture discussions, it was definitely bedtime for everyone. Paul and Rosanna and the children soon headed out to spend the night at the family home with her siblings in their Mem's absence.

Raymond and Laura spent the night on the couch and a recliner in Mem's room. However, when they closed their eyes, sleep escaped them. Rosanna's words left them more disturbed than they cared to admit, even to themselves.

Finally, they had to look those verses up in the Bible for themselves so they could get some sleep. Being careful not to disturb Mem from her sleep, Raymond quietly opened the drawer in the night stand and grabbed the Gideon Bible. He quickly found the passages Rosanna had referenced.

"Wow! The things they mentioned are literally right in here," Raymond confirmed as he read the Bible. "What else have we been missing?" He asked Laura as he headed back to his nest of blankets on the couch.

"Well, some of it is not new to me. I've heard Rosanna talk about it before, but I don't understand all of it," Laura replied.

"Maybe we'd better learn more about it if it was so important to your mem," said Raymond. "We know she doesn't freely give heed to biblical discussions from just anybody."

"Well, do we want to turn out like Paul and Rosanna? It would change our lives forever," Laura warned.

"Yeah, I suppose you're right. We should be careful, sometimes it's hard to unlearn things!" He smiled and soon drifted into dreamland.

In her excitement, sleep seemed to escape Rosanna as well that night.

Her mind was racing - *Would Mem really take those Scriptures to heart? Only God can give Mem understanding and draw her to Himself. Would she yield her heart to the Savior? Would Mem get the sleep and rest she so desperately needed, or would she lie awake thinking about it too?*

Rosanna prayed fervently for her mem's spiritual and physical condition before drifting off to sleep after midnight.

After her short night's sleep Rosanna rose early with an urge to hurry over to the hospital to see how Mem was doing. Since Hannah and Micah were still asleep, Paul decided he would bring them to the hospital after breakfast.

When Rosanna walked past the hospital waiting room, all was quiet and empty, except for a few lone strangers. She imagined that they were probably waiting to see family as well. She headed straight to her Mem's room, eager to see how she survived the night.

Mem was awake, and a nurse told her that the doctor would be in soon to check on her condition.

Raymond and Laura were up early as well and soon left for the cafeteria to get a coffee and donut.

"How was your night, Mem?" Rosanna asked.

"Not too bad, I slept better than usual," she said with a smile.

"I'm glad to hear that!" Rosanna said, wondering what Mem's smile was implying. She waited, eager for her to continue.

"Were you able to sleep most of the night?" Rosanna probed.

"Well, honestly, I thought about those Scriptures again for a long time after you left last night. I never imagined letting myself believe any biblical teachings other than what I've been taught all my life, but I couldn't find peace until I talked to God about it.

"Finally, I simply prayed and asked Him to forgive me and be my Savior. He gave me peace, Rosanna. And now I'm not afraid to go when my life is over here on earth. I see it's all because of what Jesus has done for me!"

Rosanna's heart nearly leapt right out of her chest at the sound of those words - words she didn't know if she would ever hear from her mem. She struggled to contain her emotions!

"Yes, Mem, that's what the Bible tells us! I am extremely happy for you, and thankful that you made peace with God last night!

"Your name is written in the Lamb's Book of Life now! We will live together with Him forever, instead of being separated from Him forever!" Rosanna added excitedly.

"Yes! I'm so grateful for His mercy in giving me one more opportunity to receive His gift of eternal life," Mem smiled misty eyed.

Twenty-six
CHAPTER 26

Three long weeks after her accident, Mem was back home and recovering well. Paul and Rosanna's family had already returned home after the first week.

Not only was Mem feeling much better physically, but her heart felt lighter and free as well, she admitted. She longed to grow through God's Word and was already enjoying her daily Bible study time.

Rosanna wondered what her mem's Amish future would hold and had warned her that she could encounter some turbulence along the way. And indeed, Mem had already sensed the beginning of a complicated future when Laura approached her about listening to Rosanna's "jargon from Clemens."

"Dat had said Clemen's teachings were not in line with the Amish teachings and way of life," she often reminded Mem.

"But, Laura, I cannot deny the peace I have in my heart. Maybe you need to study the Bible for yourself and see if Clemens is telling the truth," Mem suggested, praying that at least the thought had been planted in Laura's mind.

"Raymond and I intend to keep our promise we made to the church at baptism. How can anyone simply turn their back to it and claim God is leading them to do so?" Laura asked, slightly agitated.

"Well, keep in mind, God won't hold us to a faulty promise made in ignorance. It is vitally important to not reject the truth God wants to show you. Don't close your eyes and ears to everything unfamiliar without first comparing it to God's Word. I made that mistake myself for far too long. You don't want to miss any biblical Truths that could affect your eternal destiny," Mem warned her again.

"We can't help but believe it is dangerous to even listen to other teachings contrary to the preaching we hear at church. When we see what happens to others who give an ear to the so-called 'new truths', we are even more convinced it is not the path we should be pursuing," Laura argued.

"I understand where you're coming from - I used to think the same way. But I realize now that I was wrong. I'll pray for you and Raymond. Keep seeking God's will," Mem said lovingly.

* * * *

Paul and Rosanna's family visited Mem and the children again on Thanksgiving Day. By then, Mem better understood from experience what Rosanna had endured as a teenager when she believed *new* Bible Truths contrary to the Amish teachings. She wept as she apologized to Rosanna for all the agony and misery they had caused her at the most difficult and lonely time in her life.

Rosanna gladly granted forgiveness and comfort as she wiped tears of joy for the miracle God had done in Mem's heart!

"We can now rejoice together!" she told Mem with great delight. "It's like Luke 10:20 says, '... *but rather rejoice, because your names are written in heaven.*'"

Paul and Rosanna promised Mem she would never regret her decision to trust Christ as her Savior, no matter the earthly consequences. Psalm 27:1 soon became Mem's favorite Bible verse, *The Lord is my light and my salvation;*

Whom shall I fear? The Lord is the strength of my life; of whom shall I be afraid?

Thanksgiving Day took on a new significance that year! It was the first time since Rosanna had left home that Mem welcomed all the children to attend their family Thanksgiving dinner.

Reluctantly, Raymond and Laura attended as well. They disagreed with Mem's choice of welcoming the wayward siblings since their bishop would not readily encourage such practices. However, they presumed he would allow them grace this time since it was only for their own family.

Everyone in attendance that day was bursting with a secret to which Mem was absolutely clueless.

In the late afternoon, a car slowly entered the driveway. Mem was preoccupied with helping the girls prepare a delicious feast as she briefly glanced out the window. "What? An egg customer on a holiday?" She turned to place the green bean casserole in the oven. "Someone better take care of him," she instructed.

She was slicing the homemade bread when she heard — "Mem, there is someone on the porch who wants to see you!"

"What? It's not an egg customer?" She questioned. *Who would stop by today? It's a holiday!*

Wiping her hands on her apron, she limped over to the door, still suffering the after effects of her accident.

At the door she paused, speechless. Her mouth dropped open when she recognized him!

"Clemens! I can't believe my eyes! Is it really you? Come in!"

After a hardy handshake, he stepped inside, laughing in utter amazement. He could not imagine this was the same cousin he had met a few years ago.

She soon became aware that Clemens had been invited, and the surprise was only on her. The family gathered around the two, mingling their tears and laughter. Nobody even seemed to notice Raymond and Laura who kept their distance and gave him a cold shoulder.

As the evening continued, the burden on Mem's heart finally got the best of her. Calling Clemens aside, she said, "I must apologize for not welcoming you with respect years ago when you came to visit us. I see now that you were concerned for our souls. Thank you for your faithful witness, even when you were rejected. You have inspired a change in the eternal destiny of at least some of our family so far! Please, pray for the rest of the family," she pleaded. "We will surely need it in the coming days!"

"I hold nothing against you," he beamed. "God used it for His glory!

"You can't comprehend how it thrills my heart to know the seed of the Gospel was not planted in vain. At the time, I assumed it *fell by the wayside.* However, God, in His goodness, protected the ground and nurtured the seed until it brought forth its intended purpose — reconciliation with God and everlasting life," Clemens said, his heart overflowing with joy and gratitude to the Lord!

Before Clemens left later that evening, he assured the family he would pray for all of them and would stop by to visit them whenever he was in the area.

"Please do!" Mem insisted, which was like music to Rosanna's ears!

Laura's jaws dropped. *It doesn't sound like Mem! Why this drastic transformation in Mem's perspective toward Clemens, and life in general?* She felt herself slowly slipping out of the family loop.

On his way out the door, Clemens paused as if in thought. "Yes, God works in mysterious ways, even through a curious teenager's eavesdropping," he chuckled, winking at Rosanna.

"Thank you, Clemens," she beamed, her heart bursting with joy and praise to the Lord!

Rosanna was certain only God could perfectly reconcile a broken relationship between a "wanna-be-perfect" Amish mem and her "rebel" teenage daughter. Yet her heart was broken that Raymond and Laura chose to remain steadfastly loyal to the Amish religion and traditions, and would consequently miss out on many future family reunions, weddings, and holiday gatherings.

The painful vacancy of this "missing piece" in Mem's heart was a constant reminder of the daughter who remained faithful to the Amish teachings of her childhood. *Must my heart remain forever broken?* Oh, how she longed to have Laura join Rosanna and the rest of the adult siblings in the choice to become part of the truly perfect family - God's family, redeemed by the blood of Christ!

Forasmuch as ye know that ye were not redeemed with corruptible things, as silver and gold, from your vain conversation received by tradition from your fathers; But with the precious blood of Christ, as of a lamb without blemish and without spot. 1 Peter 1:18-19

ABOUT THE AUTHOR

Mary Schrock was born into an Amish family and grew up in an Old Order Amish community. She joined the church, married an Amish young man, and together they had two children while living in the Amish culture and religion.

It was not until she was twenty-six years old that Mary and her husband realized some surprising truths about the Amish religion. This realization resulted in them leaving all they had ever known and enter the "English" world with a new Hope and purpose in life.

In Mary's autobiography, *The Greater Inheritance*, she beautifully tells the story of her childhood, growing up years, courtship and early married life, and their journey to find the Truth.

www.MarySchrockBooks.com

MARY'S AUTOBIOGRAPHY

The Greater Inheritance

Gain an eye-opening view of the Amish culture, lifestyle, and religion as you read this true story of Mary's Amish family's traumatic journey to the Truth.

Available online at www.MarySchrockBooks.com

Contact: MarySchrockBooks@gmail.com